"Woody Allen once said, 'I'm not afraid of dying. I just don't want to be there when it happens.' For those of us who will be there when it happens, Kelvin Chin is providing insight, caring support and a warm life philosophy."

~ Pen Densham, Oscar Nominated Filmmaker

"This is a very impressive work and something I will read and reread throughout this life. Many thanks for writing it. I think everyone who reads it will forever be changed no matter their beliefs. Small or large, no matter. It will stick."

~ Greg Berning, Congressional Campaign
Senior Staff and Energy Executive

"Just finished the book. Once I got going I couldn't put it down. Very insightful. Loved the personal stories. Everyone can benefit from it."

~ Donna Carpenter,
Recent Widow and Caregiver

"Your book is not like others that are out there, it is going to make a difference because it is going to really cause people to think, to question, to be more tolerant, and even ask questions about things they were taught. It and you will have an impact! A much needed book on more than fear, but of really living."

~ Diane Rousseau, PhD

"Kelvin provides us a lens through which to see our fears more clearly. He teases out the various options about what may happen to us at the time of death and the role that cognition may, or may not, play in that arena. Since we are not born with an "on/off" switch, it seems reasonable to continue on to a broader societal discussion of the management of suffering, and what a humane ending of life will look like as a standard practice in the field of medicine. This book will help you to frame these discussions with an open mind, heart and spirit."

~ Rev. Robert J. Wagener, MA, MDiv,
Hospice and University Chaplain

"I found it fascinating. Got me thinking about my own beliefs and fears surrounding death. I appreciate how you have offered different alternatives and possible belief systems without judgment and with objectivity. I'm confident that your thoughts and writings will be shared with many and serve as a catalyst for people to be more open to discussions about death. Love your encouragement for people to turn within and live in the present. Such good advice!"

~ Gary Saint Denis, Former Chairman &
Co-Founder, 1-800-DENTIST

"There are so many folks I'd love to give this book to. It is one of those books that makes you think, 'How is it possible no one has done this before.' It feels like the most natural information when presented as Kelvin does, saying things that have long needed to be said and laid out. This is really a book of life — a guide of sorts — disguised as a book about death. It holds pearls of wisdom for a more balanced and insightful life. It helps bridge a gap in conversation with others. It gives you an overview of a subject long held at arms-length that no one prior has laid out so clearly and concisely. It may be the best gift to offer to loved ones for a long time."

~ Mary Hickey Randall

"Beautiful, Kelvin. Clear, calming and compassionate... so much so that it speaks directly to both the analytical mind and the heart in a way that's so calming. Awesome!"

~ Laura Tateishi Selis

"Designed to embrace and respect all beliefs and religions, this captivating and informative book masterfully guides one's mind and thought processes to uncharted territory. Kelvin Chin eloquently guides his readers to explore their own personal views surrounding what (at some point in all our lives) we'll inevitably face...dying and death. A must read for caregivers and people of all ages!"

~ Deanna Hunt

"I love your voice in your book: I truly felt that you were in the room with me. It has helped me deal with the loss of my hero, my Father. I felt like I had a good friend guiding me through the hardest time of my life. I am so grateful that this book has been here to guide me through my grief and to help me understand and accept his death and move on from this pain."

~ Maria Barr

Overcoming the Fear of Death

Overcoming the Fear of Death

Through Each of the
4 Main Belief Systems

Kelvin H. Chin

Overcoming the Fear of Death:
Through Each of the 4 Main Belief Systems
Kelvin H. Chin

Copyright © 2016 by Kelvin H. Chin
All Rights Reserved

For permission requests, please contact the author at
www.OvercomingTheFearOfDeath.org

Ordering Information

Quantity Sales. Special discounts are available on quantity purchases by hospices, retirement communities, schools, associations, and others. For details, contact the Foundation at the above website.

Individual Sales. This book is available for purchase in print, e-book, and audiobook from Amazon, bookstores, and through the links on the last page of this book using the QR code.

Published in the United States by Aurelian Press.
ISBN 978-0-9977174-0-2

First Edition

Jacket design: Simon Avery
Interior design: Susan Veach
Book Manager: Kathryn Bartman

To all those who may be inspired to help others

be freed from the limiting effects of fear...

*"It is not the end of the physical body
that should worry us.
Rather, our concern must be to live
while we're alive — to release our inner selves
from the spiritual death that comes with
living behind a façade
designed to conform to external definitions
of who and what we are."*

— Elisabeth Kübler-Ross

*"It is not death that a man should fear, but he
should fear never beginning to live."*

— Marcus Aurelius

CONTENTS

Chapter 1
My Approach to
Overcoming the Fear of Death

Chapter 2
Fear of Death

Chapter 3
Our Objectives

Chapter 4
"Fight or Flight" Response

Chapter 5
Understanding *Along With* the
Opposite of "Fight or Flight"

Chapter 6
The 4 Main Belief Systems
About Death — an Overview

Chapter 7
The First Belief System

Chapter 8
The Second Belief System

Chapter 9
The Third Belief System

Chapter 10
Recognition Memories

Chapter 11
The Fourth Belief System

Chapter 12
What's the Value of Past Lives?

Chapter 13
Other Values of Past Life Memories

Chapter 14
Final Thoughts

Epilogue

Appendix I

Appendix II

Appendix III

Acknowledgments

First, I would like to thank the many friends and family who allowed me to include in this book their personal stories of their experiences with death and dying. Your sharing of these experiences will impact the lives of many in a positive and freeing way.

A special thanks to my friend Charlie Donahue who taught many of us who were fortunate to teach alongside him in the 1970's his model of helping people look at the mind and its interrelation with the world, and explain that abstract concept in more easily understandable terms to the everyday person on the street.

I would like to acknowledge Maharishi Mahesh Yogi who reminded me how to "turn within" when I was 19 years old, as well as my former French professor at Dartmouth, John A. Rassias who first encouraged me to begin to apply my perspective about the mind in the context of varying beliefs and world views through the prism of French playwrights, philosophers, and religious thinkers. I send my deepest thanks to them, who are both now 'on the other side.'

Words cannot fully capture the appreciation I would like to express to my close friends, who have acted in so many roles — editors, idea sounding boards, camera operators — not just with this book project but throughout my life…George, Greg, Kamin, Matt, Steve, Jeff and Ken.

And, to my children Jesse and Samantha, both beautiful inside and out, souls whose waters run deep and clear.

My love and heartfelt thanks to my life partner, Kim Carpenter, who is amazing, powerful and wise, and yet somehow finds my idiosyncrasies amusing.

Finally, I thank all of you who have touched me throughout my life — whether for brief or long moments, in business or pleasure, in my childhood or in my adult life. Because relationships help us learn more about who we are, so I thank you each deeply for having passed something along to me in that process, for having enriched my life, and so that I have been able to pass along some of that — which I have gleaned from you — to others in my life.

Preface

*What is death? Is it the end, the beginning,
or a transition?*

*Why are we so afraid of death?
After all, death is inevitable.*

My hope is that this book will help us rethink both how we respond to the death of a loved one, and how we think about our own death.

It doesn't matter what your beliefs are about death or about religion. This book embraces all beliefs about death and dying, and will explore it from the many perspectives that people from around the world — from all cultures and religions — have about it. Essentially, every belief someone may have about death will fall somewhere in the belief systems we will discuss.

Everyone will be represented in the discussion.

There are many books already written on the many cultures and religions that exist throughout the world. This book focuses on the underlying beliefs that cut across those many cultures and religions.

We will discuss:

The 4 Main Belief Systems About Death:
1) No Belief in Afterlife
2) Afraid of Heaven or Hell
3) Looking Forward to Heaven
4) Belief in Past Lives

The insights in this book should assist us in understanding death more clearly and aligning that understanding more accurately with each of our respective belief systems — whatever they may be.

To do this, we will look at the death and dying process through the lens of our own respective belief systems. And by focusing on one belief system at a time, not only will each of us develop greater clarity and understanding about our own views on death and dying, but also we will develop a sensitivity and sensibility for how others think about death — others who may have very different belief systems from ours — thereby helping us each to be better caregivers for others, whether they share our beliefs about death or not.

Because regardless of whether we are a professional caregiver — a doctor, nurse, therapist, home healthcare or hospice worker — or whether we are "just regular people going about our daily lives" — we all will someday find ourselves caring for loved ones who are at the end of life. There is no escaping that. And when that time inevitably comes, we all can benefit from having a greater, more sensitive understanding of how we each view death and dying.

And what is the overarching effect of increasing that understanding and sensibility about death?

It will help us to reduce and eventually overcome the fear of death. To free up otherwise wasted energy that can be refocused to better use in our daily lives. To help us live more enjoyable and productive lives.

I truly hope this book helps you in your life journey.

Kelvin H. Chin
February 17, 2016
Austin, Texas

Special Note to Caregivers...

As caregivers, whether we are professional ones or not, we are there to support. Not to convince or persuade our patients or loved ones of our beliefs about death or dying. At those moments — when we are at their bedside — our role is to set aside our beliefs. Our job is to "be there" with them. Fully. And that means accepting them *for who they are* — including their beliefs about death, however different they may be from *ours*.

To do that effectively and genuinely, we must be comfortable with our own beliefs about death — and ideally with our own fears about death — as well as be aware and cognizant of their beliefs. We must at least be aware enough to navigate their beliefs to the degree discussed in this book. That does not mean we need to understand all the details — whether culturally or religiously — of their beliefs about death and dying. But it does mean that we need to be comfortable enough with the full range of beliefs about death, as to make them feel comfortable in our acceptant attitude — which will then be reflected in our nonverbal behavior and verbal communications with them.

If we are at least successful to that level, then they will feel our genuine acceptance of their beliefs. They will feel our love for them in that way. And they will feel healed by us, by that mere interjection of unspoken understanding and acceptance.

And we will — that much more fully — have done our job as a caregiver.

We will have then helped that patient or loved one ease through the dying process in a way that no amount of money or materiality can measure. We will have given them a gift easing their pain and suffering, and increasing their comfort from within that should be an integral part of how we — in our humanity — treat each other at that very special moment in our life.

Chapter 1

My Approach to Overcoming the Fear of Death

My Approach

I have the same belief about death as I do about birth. It's going to happen. It's inevitable. There is no stopping it.

Most of you probably share that same belief. You might even call it a simple observation.

But those very obvious types of beliefs about death are not what I'm going to talk about in this book.

Instead, I'm going to discuss the "Four Main Belief Systems" that everyone has about death. These belief systems are held by the followers of every religion or spiritual group, and are found in every culture on the planet.

In short, everyone is covered by these Four Main Belief Systems about death.

And I'm going to show how no matter what your belief system is, you can reduce and even eliminate or overcome your fear of death.

But first, before we get started, let me give you a sense of how I approach this seemingly daunting, sometimes morbid and fear-invoking topic.

I often run into people in elevators and planes as I travel the world talking about death and dying, and they ask me, "What do you do?" So, after I tell them that I help people overcome their fear of death (if they haven't already run away waving their arms saying, "Whoa, I don't want to think about that, it scares me too much!"), then this often leads to a conversation that starts with my perspective on the subject.

The first thing I usually say is that I want to make it crystal clear to everybody that while we are talking about something that's obviously a fairly serious subject, I take an approach towards it that's very down to earth, and to the extent that it's possible, a little bit lighter in the way we talk about death and dying. That's the way I lean — because I want to encourage more discussion and thought about death.

I think a big part of the issue — a big problem quite frankly that we as a culture have — is not talking about death and dying. Just even talking about it is a good thing, just discussing ideas, beliefs about it, perceptions, maybe even discussing experiences that some people may have had related to themselves or their loved ones.

This would be a significant advance over the current practice and behavior.

Instead, we tell people: "Don't talk about that here, especially not in front of the children," or "I don't want to hear about *that!*" or "Don't be a 'downer'...who wants to talk about that...let's have fun instead."

Okay, I understand and agree that there is a time and place for everything. And that maybe discussing death and dying at your birthday party is not the best place. But as a culture, we have created too many 'good excuses' to avoid it. And so we do.

This is not healthy. It increases the mystery and misunderstandings surrounding death. And the mystery and misunderstandings surrounding death just lead to more unnecessary fear.

So, our job as a culture should be to de-mystify death. And that starts by talking about it, sharing ideas, and hopefully increasing our understanding about it.

Talking about death and dying would change how we treat each other when it comes to death and dying. It would change how we create spaces to tend to our sick members of our communities — it would change the architecture of our healthcare facilities, the lighting, the air, the ambience.

It would change how we talk to them, or with them. It would change how we tend to the needs of our sick brothers and sisters in the world community.

In this book, we're going to cover a lot of different areas, topics and issues related to death and dying, and I think you'll get a sense pretty quickly how I approach this whole discussion. But at its essence, I view this book and the work our Foundation does as a catalyst for these important conversations that we as a world society need to be having.

Start Young

First, I think we need to start talking more openly about death and dying with our children. I don't think there is an age at which it's too young to discuss. It's how you do it that's important.

Speaking about death and dying with our children as a natural progression of living life should become the norm. It should not be treated as some scary event. And if you as a parent think of it as a scary event, then you need to first address your own fears before discussing this area with your children. That would be ideal. Responsible parenting would suggest that you work immediately on your own fears so that you don't inadvertently transfer them to your children.

Ask for help. Perhaps you have friends who are not fearful of discussing death and dying with their kids. Ask them how they did it. Seek out your friends' advice.

And when your friends or relatives are dying, take that as an opportunity to explain what is going on to your children. Do not hide it from them. You do them and yourselves a disservice if you do that.

When my dad was ill, we didn't hide it from our children. He had been diagnosed and treated for colon cancer in 1996. However, it resurfaced in a blood test in 1998. Fortunately he was with us for another year before he passed away.

During that year, my dad worked full-time, driving every day from his condominium complex in Torrance, California to his post-retirement job in Beverly Hills as the office manager at Bikram's flagship yoga studio. Often he would visit us — especially his two grandchildren Jesse and Samantha — in Mar Vista, a section of Los Angeles adjacent to Venice, after he finished work on the weekends.

Our children — then 9 years old and 4 years old — gradually witnessed my dad's health decline over those subsequent 12 months. We had told them of his illness, and that he was dying.

More and more frequently, they saw him fall asleep...at first to take a short nap just when he arrived after the 20-minute drive from his office, then later, longer naps. Eventually the falling asleep would happen mid-stream during conversations at the dining room table, and even during meals.

Our kids saw it all. Nothing was hidden from them.

Grandpa would even tell them that he would sometimes have to pull his car over to the side of the road on Sepulveda Boulevard, on his way to work from Torrance to Beverly Hills, to take a nap. Sometimes he would sleep for 45 minutes in his car before he could be awake enough to finish the drive. (At least he was self-aware enough to put his and others' safety first when he felt tired! A good lesson for the kids to hear.)

When my dad couldn't get himself out of bed, my sister Lorinda, my buddy Steve and I moved him to our house. He died there 36 hours later.

But during that time, while he slept most of the time in our living room, cared for by a 24/7 hospice nurse, our children were with him. They saw the many dozens of people come to say their last goodbyes to my dad — his engineer friends from Hughes Aircraft in El Segundo, his Bikram Yoga students and teachers whose teacher trainings he had organized, and the diverse mix of others ranging from Chinese-only speaking distant relatives who hadn't seen him in 60 years to nightclub dancers. Our children saw the tears and felt the waves of sadness in the room. And they saw how the warm and respectful hospice nurse cared for him throughout.

When he died on January 28, 1999 at 1:45 AM, we woke the kids up to come see his body and experience their grandpa after he had passed — to experience that final stage of the dying process. The hospice nurse had helped us move his body from the wheelchair to the hospital bed we rented, and my siblings and their families, and our children and their mom gathered around my dad's shell.

And our kids kissed their grandpa on the forehead 'goodbye.'

That was how we handled the death of my dad with our children. You of course need to decide how to do it with your kids.

But here are a few suggestions.

Use that opportunity, while they are still alive but perhaps ill, to express to your children how much you enjoy that loved one in your life, celebrate what they have accomplished and how they did it, and who they are. Tell them stories about their grandpa, about their eccentric aunt, or whomever. Even if your children weren't around when those events occurred, they will feel your enthusiasm, your emotional connection with that loved one. And if their grandpa is still lucid, get him involved in telling the stories to your children to the extent he is able.

That's what will 'touch' your children. They will sense your security, your calmness and comfort. And then, they will not find death and dying fearful or abnormal.

Your children will take your lead. They will then focus their attention on those positive attributes about that person's life, and about the normality of death (no matter how it came about) as the end of that loved one's life — regardless of how short or long it was.

And that lesson will stay with your children their entire lives.

Think of it as a gift you as a parent are giving to your children…and to their children. There is no greater gift than that of understanding and of freeing them from the binding and limiting effects of fear. This is perhaps the greatest legacy we could leave our children.

Prepare Loved Ones

The Boy Scout motto is "Be Prepared." The correlate to that is to "prepare others."

If you know that a loved one is ill, don't wait until they are dying to tell others about the news. Tell the rest of the family sooner rather than later that Uncle Frederick fell and hurt himself falling off a horse. Don't wait until his injury turns into some life-threatening event before you share the news with family members.

No one benefits from being shocked at bad news. We all assimilate bad news easier in smaller, more gradually administered doses. Do the same with news about illness or injury — whether life-threatening or not.

Of course the situation to be avoided, if at all possible, is suddenly telling friends and family the news that someone died. Nevertheless, sometimes that happens, either through illness or accident. And we need to manage talking about it as best we can.

But if we have practiced with our children when they were young, we will have had plenty of years of honing our communications skills on this sensitive subject, and the leap of understanding and assimilation will be a less daunting challenge — no matter how young or old our audience.

Understanding versus Inspiration

The most common way most people handle issues around death and dying is what I refer to as the "Inspirational Approach."

Its objective is to help us feel some immediate relief. And it does.

For example, when someone is experiencing the loss of a loved one or a fear of dying oneself, friends often say, "Don't worry, she's in a better place now, she's at peace…" or "You'll be Ok, don't worry about the fears you have, they'll pass — you'll be fine."

And we feel better, perhaps — temporarily. So, it does work. Just not for very long. And it tends to be case specific. It is not usually transferrable to another situation. By the time the next situation arises, you are back at 'square one' again.

That is the most common approach out there. And there are many seminars offered and articles written about helping people with death and dying issues, but if you look beneath the surface of what they are saying and recommending, basically it's a variation on that same inspirational message.

And, keep in mind, there is nothing wrong with that approach. I use it myself at times. In certain situations, it is the appropriate approach.

My point is that, while it is the most common approach in our culture to dealing with death and dying, it is not the only approach.

The approach I will be taking in this book is different. We will be taking the "Understanding Approach."

By looking closely at each of the Four Main Belief Systems about death, by clarifying our fears about death and dying, and by exploring insights and understandings about death that may have been outside our normal thinking, we will perhaps shed new light on this subject.

And by shedding new light on this, we may find ourselves loosening a bit, feeling more freedom from the previously binding and limiting effects of the fear of death.

My experience over the past thirty years helping people with death and dying issues is that increasing their *understanding* tends to be more long lasting and is more transferrable from situation to situation.

And one might say that the experience of 'freedom from fear' is the ultimate inspiration.

Chapter 2

Fear of Death

The Elephant in the Room

For some of you, it may have taken a lot of courage to buy this book.

I wonder how many of you stood in the bookstore in front of the bookshelf, or stared at your computer monitor at one of the book websites and were thinking, "Oh, should I buy it? Or, will it scare me even more? Should I just continue to try to *not* think about death?"

Seriously, I'm certain that a number of you felt that way, and that's totally fine. You should feel comfortable with that 'feeling of being uncomfortable' because I think it's a very normal thing for many of us in our culture to feel uncomfortable about death and the dying process.

Let's talk about that.

It's totally normal.

There's nothing at all abnormal about feeling uncomfortable about death, and wanting to *not* think about it. Yet, no matter how much you want to avoid thinking about it, you inevitably *do* think about it.

We think — when I say "we," I mean we as a culture — a lot more about death and dying than people will admit in their private moments. It's there. For many, it's always there. In the background.

It's like the elephant in the room, isn't it?

You know, the "elephant in the room" analogy?

It's as if there is this huge elephant standing over there in the corner of the room — how much does an elephant weigh? It weighs a lot — they can weigh as much as 14,000 pounds! That's 7 tons. It's big, physically big. It's huge — and they can be as tall as 13 feet from shoulder to toe. They are quite literally the largest land animal on the planet.

You cannot miss the fact that it's in the room, but if you don't look over there, you think maybe it'll go away — maybe, just maybe, it will disappear.

But…the elephant is still there.

The Big One

Fear is like that. It's like that elephant in the room.

And, the big one — the big fear — is the "Fear of Death."

I've chosen, through my Foundation's work, to start talking and increasing our understanding about the fear of death, because it's 'the Big One.' It's the one where people sometimes say, "Oh no, I don't think about death. I'm not afraid of death," and then you find out when either a loved one of theirs (or perhaps themselves) starts having to deal with their own issues of dying, then that's when it starts to come up for them.

It has been there for them the whole time. They have just fooled themselves into thinking that since they skirted the issue in their conscious mind most of the time, that it hasn't been there. But it has been there, at least on a subconscious level.

Eventually the fear of death appears — with all its inherent power, its gripping and, in some cases, its crippling effects on us. It's been dormant, it's been lying there — it's there — but they haven't been thinking about it. So, they incorrectly think they have not been affected by it.

I'm just encouraging people to talk about death, to think about it. This is the first step — you should think about reading this book with that objective in mind.

The Effect of Fear

Fear contracts us. It restricts our creativity.

Sometimes fear even causes us to do things that may not be so good for us. People may abuse drugs to escape from their problems, or stay in an unhealthy relationship out of their fear to explore something they are unfamiliar with, or hold themselves back from applying for that better job due to their fear of new things or fear of failure.

Fear is *not* a good thing — it limits us and drains our energy.

So, I was thinking a long time ago — wouldn't it be great if we could somehow free up the energy that's associated with all that fear — instead of wasting it worrying about this, and worrying about that. And in this case, worrying about the fear of death, and worrying about the fear of dying and the process of dying.

Instead, imagine if we could free up some of that energy so that we could use that energy more productively — maybe in our relationships with other people, maybe to do our jobs better, maybe to come up with some creative new idea, some invention — perhaps come up with a cure for cancer. In other words, use that energy in a much more productive way for ourselves individually and for our society as a whole.

There is no end to the areas of our lives we could better direct that energy to, instead of wasting it on fear — especially if that fear could be reduced and dispensed with in a relatively short period of time through something as painless as increasing our understanding about the object of our fear — death.

Chapter 3

Our Objectives

Living In The Present

The larger mission of our foundation — the Overcoming the Fear of Death Foundation — is all about living life now — living better, more productively — *here and now*.

See, so it really doesn't matter what your belief system is.

Whether you believe that you're going to come back life-after-life for eternity, it doesn't matter. We're all still living *right here, right now*.

Or alternatively, if you believe that, like my father did — and we'll talk about some of my father's stories in a minute — whether you believe in his belief system which was: "When the body dies, the mind dies — it shuts off, 'Throw the dirt on me, I'm done'...." (he used to say) — the message is still the same —

"Live life *now* in the continual present."

The Foundation essentially is all about improving our quality of life now, living life now. That's the focus. That's really why I created the Foundation.

History of Our Foundation — My Mom's Death

Just a little history…

People frequently ask me how I got into this area, and why I started this Foundation.

What 'kick-started' my interest in death and dying and their related issues?

The death of my mom.

She was fairly young, in her mid-50's, and I was in my third year of law school at the time. Even now, many years later, every time I tell this I get a little choked up — you see, sadness over the loss of a loved one is normal — it is a reflection of how deep our relationship with them was.

When she died, it was really difficult for me to get my mind around. Suffice it to say that in my own very personal way, I suffered. I suffered emotionally when she was dying and then again after she died, when I experienced the pain of losing her.

It was difficult for me to see her in the hospital in such pain and obviously dying. We all knew she was dying imminently — it was just a matter of time, and we knew it would be a short time, given the oncologist's prognosis and description of her brain as "having so many malignant tumors that it looked like raisin bread…."

I would bring my law books to study next to her bed sometimes, and she would tell me, "Go study, don't worry about me…." Even though the drive from Chestnut Hill, where I lived and was attending law school, to her hospital in Walpole, Massachusetts was only a 45-minute drive, I visited her only sporadically. It was too emotionally painful for me. I sort of shut down emotionally. My first marriage suffered further from it, and I managed to graduate from law school and do my part-time job at a Boston law firm — but just barely.

(Some of you may be saying, "Ok, well how do I handle that? How do I overcome that pain and suffering?" I get into that in my second book — I want to stay focused here on the "fear of death," but I acknowledge that these related fears are also obviously important as well.)

My mom was gone in a matter of months.

She was a smoker. I remember when I was in college I once asked her, "When did you start smoking, Mom?"

She said she was 11 years old when she started smoking in Chinatown in Boston, and I was shocked, "11 years old?!" I was probably 20 years old when she told me that.

Today I'm a few years older than that, and I have a 27-year-old son and a 21-year-old daughter. And so now I have a much better sensibility for what "11 years old" is for a child to start smoking — chain smoking at 11 years old.

It shocks me even more now.

Anyway, she smoked for 40 years and then she died.

It was difficult for me. Law school was difficult enough without having to deal with my mom's sudden death. I managed to keep it together enough to go to classes and to my part-time investigator and law clerk job at the Boston law firm, but it was very difficult for me to get my mind wrapped around this whole thing, the relatively sudden death of my mom.

I basically 'self-helped' my way through this intense process. I embraced her amazing life, all that she did for us in the family and for her friends and acquaintances. And I embraced my sadness over her not being able to be with me when I graduated law school, and more significantly my sadness over her just not being around any more.

I cried a lot in the privacy of my bedroom. Every time I would sit to meditate twice a day, it seemed like that intention to 'let go' in meditation was enough to just open my emotional flood gates — and I cried, sobbing, feeling the deep sadness and loss. So, I just let myself be in that state, without judging it, and afterwards, maybe 20-30 minutes or more later, I would get up and feel 'lighter,' less stressed, though still sad. But much less overwhelmed with sadness. And because of that experience, I redefined how I thought of meditation…that was my meditation at that time… crying and letting go.

Gradually, over the subsequent weeks and months, I began to come to terms with her death — deep within myself.

It was my toughest, most challenging self-help process.

Then, you know how people will often ask you, "So how are you doing today?" and most people just answer, "Oh, I'm doing fine. I'm doing great…" — even if you're not, because you usually don't want to get into it. You don't want to get into how you're really feeling inside — it's either too private, or you don't want to get upset, or maybe you're just too busy and need to get to an appointment.

But then, when people asked me that, I started saying, "You know what, my mom just died," and they would then open up and say, "Whoa. My grandmother just died, [or] my brother just died, [or] my father just…"

People started disclosing their personal, private, intimate stories and feelings to me, just from my saying, "Oh, my mom just died."

Self-disclosure can often do that — it opens people up to also disclose to you. They feel safe because you've taken the first step of risking something personal with them. A bridge of trust is quickly built, a bond even if only temporary is immediately created.

Interestingly, if I had said what I usually said — and what most people say — "Oh, I'm doing fine," when I really wasn't fine, that would not have happened.

People started telling me their stories and feelings about death and dying.

So, little by little, gradually what happened was that nights and weekends I was occasionally on the phone starting to help people deal with their death and dying issues — just for free. People would call me up, and this went on for years, throughout my legal services and corporate career working with Fortune 500 companies and others.

I did my day-job for decades, but every once in a while on nights and weekends people would call me from all over the country and they would just say, "Hey, Kel, a friend of yours referred me, and I want to talk with you about something...."

That was the genesis historically of what got me started with this type of work and eventually inspired me to create my Foundation.

So...I have been 'on the other side' — on that emotionally difficult and dark side of death and loss of a loved one — rudderless — and now I want to share what I have learned with others.

Making Death and Dying More 'Normal'

Again, why did I create this Overcoming the Fear of Death Foundation?

We talked about one reason. One reason was freeing up energy, not wasting energy on fears in general — and specifically the 'Big One' — the fear of death and related fears.

The other reason is to try to make the whole death and dying process a little bit easier for our culture to get its minds and hearts around, and to treat it a little bit more naturally, more normally.

The Effect on Our Healthcare

Our healthcare providers have a hard enough time as it is caring for their patients' physical needs. And while responsible caregivers know their patients need more mental support, they are often ill-equipped with the knowledge of how to counsel patients and their families on death and dying. To be candid, most never got sufficient training in school. Moreover, many are still walking around and dispensing healthcare while carrying their own life burdens and personal fears about death and dying.

So, they avoid it. They focus on the medical, on the physical, on prolonging physical life. And that prolonging of physical life at any cost is generally applauded by our society. So we can't merely blame them — we as a society are complicit. We often demand it of them.

Some experts have estimated that 50 percent of our healthcare costs in the United States are spent in the last 6 months of life. This may just be part of our medical urban lore, but whatever the actual percentage, everyone agrees that it is a big number.

For example, here is one reliable statistic. In 2008, Medicare paid $55 billion just for doctor and hospital bills during the last 2 *months* of patients' lives. That was more than the total budget for the United States Department of Homeland Security, or the Department of Education.

So taking care of patients in the last 2 months of their lives, we in the United States spent almost half as much on doctor and hospital bills (just from Medicare...not including other insurance sources even!) as we spent that year on our country's entire national education programs! And to make this social narrative even more troubling, it has been estimated that 20 to 30 percent of these medical expenses may have had no meaningful impact on the patients' lives.

Whatever the metric, and however accurate the study may be — the undisputed outcome is that we are wasting money on questionable, if not futile, healthcare.

Think about it — we spend exorbitant and arguably unnecessary amounts of money in the last days of life.

Why? I think it is largely because we are a culture that values the physical life more than the mental *quality* of life.

I think we as a culture suffer because of that skewed value. We suffer emotionally and financially. And the quality of our healthcare suffers.

The Effect on Our Military

Similarly, our military is equally ill-equipped in this area.

Soldiers are not given education on death and dying. They are trained fully on how to kill. But when they are wounded, or their comrades are killed, they are at a total loss.

They are left to fend for themselves — they are left adrift by the military and healthcare systems — because our culture avoids dealing with death and dying. And often the results are tragic — battlefield deaths that could have been avoided if a soldier had not frozen up or lost focus when a comrade died next to him, suicides that are hushed up, drug addictions that are tolerated or even enabled because a better alternative is unknown, and broken families in which all the participants suffer, especially the young children.

Our culture ignores the elephant in the room.

Death is going to happen.

But I am hoping that we can at least increase the comfort level around death and dying. Because as you well know, in most cultures around the world (and maybe even for some of you right now who are reading this book) — death is not a comfortable topic.

If we can increase that comfort a little bit, it will free up that energy — people can be much more creative. They can live happier lives.

Measuring Our Fear Of Death

As I said earlier, we do think about the fear of death a lot. And as I thought about it further, I asked myself —

What's a good measure of how much people think about the fear of death?

So, I thought: "Jokes."

And I decided to Google those words. I literally plugged them into the search window — I typed "death jokes." And you know how many search results I got?

I got 65 million results.

That's a lot. There's a lot of thinking going on about death, even though people will say, "Oh, I don't think about it. It doesn't bother me. I don't think about the death thing," or whatever.

One of the jokes in particular jumped out at me... and I apologize in advance because I can't do Woody Allen's accent here, but imagine in his Brooklyn, New York accent, he says —

"I'm not afraid of death.
I just don't want to be there when it happens."

I love Woody.

And while death and dying are serious subjects, I think it is important for us — in our efforts to overcome our fears — to not get too overly serious. After all, life is to be enjoyed as best we can.

What About Clarity And Related Fears?

We will talk more about related fears later in a subsequent book, because there are a lot of people who may have little or no fear of death *itself*, but they may still have other *related fears* to the dying *process*.

However, I think it is very important to understand at the outset that in those cases it's not the "fear of death."

And you may say, "So what?"

Here's the "so what."

I think it's really important to understand clearly what our fears are of, because if we don't, we may be walking around thinking we've got six or eight fears, yet in reality, we may not actually be afraid of that many. Perhaps we are really in fact just afraid of one or two things.

It's important to understand what our fears are for at least two reasons.

One is that we're wasting all this energy thinking, "I'm afraid of death. I'm afraid of (this or that)...." — and we actually may not be, so we could immediately conserve our energy, and use it more productively by eliminating fears we don't even actually have.

The other reason is that by being more clear about our fears, it helps us be much more effective in solving those fears. We can much more readily apply the appropriate solution to get rid of those fears, reduce those fears, if we know what the fear really is.

There's a lot of confusion and conflation going on in people's minds. So I'm all about clarity, which is another reason why I think a *rational approach* to this whole death and dying area is important.

Fear of National Parks

Here is an example that may help illustrate what I mean.

Let's say somebody goes to a national park, and they look down over this cliff — approximately a mile down — and it freaks them out because it's *so far down*. And because of the fear invoked by that experience, they never *ever* want to go to a national park again. Their whole life they are afraid to go to national parks because — in their mind — if they go to a national park, they're going to be terrified.

They don't realize that the fear is not a "fear of national parks."

The fear is of *going to the Grand Canyon*, which of course, happens to be a national park. And because they conflated their fears — i.e., they combined them and mixed them up — they wasted the rest of their life not visiting and enjoying other beautiful national parks — Yellowstone, the Everglades, or other national parks that do not invoke their fear of heights.

People do that with death and dying issues all the time. So, it's important to get clear on what our fears are of.

Fixation on the Fear of Death

What if you are fixated on the fear of death?

When I have worked with people who have this fixation, typically they have already sought or are continuing to get help through the traditional channels — psychotherapists and medical professionals (allopaths (MD's, RN's), naturopaths, homeopaths, chiropractors, acupuncturists, doulas, and others). I support and encourage them to explore those avenues, and I remind them that I am not a therapist, nor a medical professional.

That said, I have found that introducing people to the full range of the Four Main Belief Systems about death that we discuss in this book not only helps them understand better how other people think, but also helps them understand better how they themselves think.

This greater understanding and more expanded exposure to other ways of thinking may even start to help that person develop a 'crowbar' to begin to loosen up the fixation they may have on the fear of death. They start to think about it differently, both consciously and subconsciously.

And just that 'thinking differently' can sometimes loosen the grip that the fear has on them.

Chapter 4

"Fight or Flight" Response

"Fight or Flight" — What It Is

This happens in all of us. It is a normal, natural part of our wiring. It's there for our survival as a species.

It's what happens in our body when that part of our autonomic nervous system called the "sympathetic nervous system" kicks in, and releases epinephrine.

Then, our adrenal gland gets triggered by hormones released by the hypothalamus, and a chemical called cortisol is produced and starts coursing through our blood stream. Our digestion slows and blood vessels constrict (except for those in our large muscles, which dilate). Our heart rate goes up, and our mouth gets dry because the lacrimal gland which regulates salivation immediately gets inhibited. We've all experienced this. It's as if we get more focused (also because our hearing lessens and vision narrows), and are getting prepared for something big to happen.

You are ready to fight for your life.

This is your body's acute stress response — thus the term "fight or flight"...

Keep in mind — it's supposed to be temporary, just to allow us to manage the situation immediately, save ourselves, then move on and get back to "normal" life.

It's a "switch" that's inside all of us that's supposed to turn on when (thousands of years ago) the saber tooth tiger was at our cave door...and we had to make a quick decision —

Do we FIGHT or do we FLEE?

So, it's there for our own good. But, as I said, it's meant to be temporary.

Negative Results...

But living in this state for long periods, or having it triggered in inappropriate situations (traffic jams, business meetings, school exams), creates negative psychological and physiological repercussions. For example, it can give rise to anger, depression, anxiety, chest pain, headaches, high blood pressure, insomnia, and a suppressed immune system. And those are just to name a few.

Without intending to, we automatically turn on this "fight or flight" mechanism too often in our lives. And because we do not know how to manage stressful situations, our bodies simply react in this way, and the switch gets turned on inside us.

And...especially for those who have a fixation on the fear of death, this trigger to the "fight or flight" response can be debilitating.

Balance is the Key

From a neurophysiological standpoint, the key is learning how to turn on the OPPOSITE of the "fight or flight" mechanism in us. This balances us.

It allows us to develop a more balanced mental, emotional and physical state so our "fight or flight" response only gets turned on when it needs to. Without having it activated when it's not supposed to.

Chapter 5

Understanding
Along With the
Opposite of "Fight or Flight"

The Ultimate Combo

This is what I refer to as the 2-pronged approach:

1) Increasing understanding about death and dying through the lens of whatever your belief system is, and

2) Learning how to turn on the opposite of the "fight or flight" response — experientially promoting the learning of any effortless technique of 'turning within' that releases the individual from the limiting effects of fears and anxieties by allowing the mind, body and emotions to relax and balance, which results in more effective thoughts and actions, and greater self-confidence, which is integral in helping people both overcome their fear of death and lead happier, more productive lives.

The 2-Pronged Approach and Why It Works

Let's look at our 2-pronged approach in greater detail, and see why it works so well.

I have found, based on 30 years of experience helping people with death and dying issues, that a combination of both understanding along with the experiential process of 'turning within' yields a much more long-lasting fear-reducing result for individuals. That is, much more long-lasting than what I described earlier in this book as the "Inspirational Approach."

Let's look at this further.

Like any other effort to improve oneself — whether it's a professional sales skills training or a personal development workshop — if the workshop focuses only on the skills learning or the "what" you should do to improve yourself, then it will likely fail. We will fail in really becoming an outstanding salesperson — we will fail at really improving ourselves in more than merely a cursory, superficial "feel good" way.

Why?

Because *the individual* is the critical component of success or failure. And if the individual's mind is weak, or the individual's body is tired, the result will be insufficient, unsatisfactory.

No matter how much content is forced upon that individual, he or she can only absorb so much. He can only integrate and synthesize as much as his 'container of information' — his mind (which is directly supported by his bodily functioning) — can process.

So, the key is how to strengthen the mind to ensure the target within that mind that we are trying to influence (in our case, the fears related to death and dying) is hit powerfully and accurately.

And the best way I've found to strengthen the mind in this integrated way with the body is by 'turning within' through meditation — connecting with oneself in that way, resting the body through that process, and allowing the neurophysiology to balance on all levels.

Importantly, the positive neurophysiological effect of the meditation also helps to begin the process of off-loading and balancing the sometimes many years of imbalances that have built up in the individual's nervous system — in both their mind and body. Perhaps stored up excesses of chemicals in their muscles and other cells are contributing to the unintended and undesirable excessive triggering of the "fight or flight" response — especially in our discussion here, related to the fear of death — and those excesses in the body can be balanced through meditation, or other 'turning within' processes.

By taking this balanced approach — mentally, emotionally, physically — the mind and body become clearer and stronger. And one's self-confidence becomes more unshakable. We feel more centered and grounded from within.

And by combining that along with increasing the understanding about death and dying through the individual's belief system, our fears dissipate and can eventually disappear.

If either "understanding" or "the 'turning within' experience of oneself" is missing, the result will be weaker, and perhaps insufficient to meet the need. In other words, we may likely miss the target. We may remain in fear.

If we only meditate, if we only 'turn within experientially' — without increasing our understanding of the issue at hand (in this case, death and dying) — we run the risk of never accomplishing our goal fully. We run the risk of simply falling into a "feel good" state of mind that is not based on substance, not based on anything "real." We never really deal with the issue we had — whether it be about death and dying, or any other related issues we may have.

On the other hand, if we only pursue the understanding route, and ignore the meditation or 'turning within experientially' route, we run the risk of only increasing our ability to understand to the extent that our mind and body will support that *in their current state.* In other words, our understanding is restricted by how clear our mind is and by how rested our body is (and by the degree of stress it can withstand) *at that particular moment.*

And remember, our bodies are closely connected to our minds and so they affect each other. If our bodies are tired, unhealthy and imbalanced, they will directly affect the clarity and the level of ability that our minds have to understand — the body will limit the mind's capacity.

So, you see, both go hand in hand.

Ideally both Understanding and Turning Within need to be there for us to fully reduce and potentially overcome our fear of death and related fears. This combination will ensure that the reduction and elimination of fears — whether they be about death and dying or any other fears — is as long-lasting and as permanent as possible.

Truly overcoming our fears is ultimately the primary way we can ensure our own happiness in life. And that, I think, is the objective of life — the pursuit of happiness.

My Belief Does Not Matter

Like I have said, this book is a first step. This is a discussion.

I'm not here to say, "You have to believe this way or that."

I'm going to talk about *all beliefs*. And you might get a sense of what my belief system is from what I talk about, but that does *not* mean that I think you should believe what I believe.

I have a belief system based on my experiences that are unique to me. You have a belief system that you are developing yourself through your lifetime that is based on your experiences, whom you come in contact with, how you understand things.

And that's the way it should be.

Thinking For Ourselves

I am a big believer in Free Will, personal choice — in individuality, in people thinking for themselves. That's why the tagline for my lectures is "a *rational* approach to freeing ourselves from the limiting effects of death."

Thinking.

I want people to think about these things more, but I'm a pragmatist. I'm a "pragmatic idealist." So while I have this idealistic side to me, I'm essentially a pragmatic guy.

I understand that this is a first step, that the expectation is not that you will read this book, and — Boom! — all your fears will be gone, or all your fears of death will be gone. No. This is a first step.

We want people to engage with each other, talk to your friends, your loved ones, talk about this more. That's what I'm encouraging. Think about it yourself, because that's where the conversation really needs to happen, *within each of us.*

So, let's start now with an overview of the Four Main Belief Systems About Death.

Chapter 6

The 4 Main Belief Systems About Death

an Overview

Ask Yourself

I'm going to talk about four different belief systems about death. And I'm going to talk about each of them in some detail. But first, ask yourself which of the four belief systems best captures *your* belief or beliefs.

I'll describe them briefly and then we'll come back and revisit each of them.

As you read each of the following belief systems, ask yourself this question —

"Do I believe that when I die, this is what is going to happen to me?"

The First Belief System

"When my body dies, my mind shuts off. The mind is connected to the body's life function, and when the body ceases, the mind ceases."

By the way, when I say mind, I mean mind in the broadest sense of the word — I do not mean mind in the typical psychological sense. So, some of you may use other words like soul, spirit, consciousness, energy, or awareness. Those are all synonymous with how I am using "mind" in this book. I prefer to use the word mind since it has no religious or cultural connotations accompanying it. It's a more neutral word. But if you want to substitute any of those other words when you read "mind" in this book, go right ahead.

The Second Belief System

"When my body dies, my mind is going to continue, and... (here's a little wrinkle on this one...) I am afraid of what might happen."

There's fear there. In other words, you're not afraid of death, but you're afraid of what may happen *afterwards.*

The Third Belief System

"When my body dies, my mind continues, but I am not afraid. There's some transition, I am not sure to what, but I am okay with it."

The Fourth Belief System

"When my body dies, my mind continues, and there's some transition, and in this case my belief system is that

during that transition period, I may actually choose to come back in another body — the idea of reincarnation, future lives, past lives."

Your Belief System

Now ask yourself — which of these four is *your* belief system?

The Range of Beliefs and Hybrids

When I give lectures on this, I ask for a show of hands at this point, and every belief system is typically represented in the audiences. Some audiences may have a higher percentage of one or two belief systems than the others, but every belief system is represented if the audience is large enough.

I should also point out that some of you may have a hybrid of any of those belief systems — that is, you may not be sure, or you may be 'hedging your bets.' You may have a mixture of two of the belief systems, or you may be 'on the fence' not sure between two of them, or sometimes you may feel one way and other times feel the other way.

A lot of people are now probably laughing — I can hear you! — hedging your bets, right? Many people hedge their bets about death because who knows for sure, right?

That's totally okay, too — so, you may have a hybrid of those belief systems. That's fine.

No Belief is More Important Than Another

It is important to understand that I am not here to promote any one belief system over another belief system — not at all. I don't care what a person's belief system is — not only about death or dying, but also religiously, if they believe in God, if they don't believe in God, or if they believe in God in this way, or if they believe in God that way.

It doesn't matter to me. I embrace all beliefs.

And remember how we talked earlier about encouraging more dialogue and discussion about death and dying in our culture?

I think a good way to do that is to increase each of our understandings about the *full range* of beliefs about death that exist in the world, so that we can each feel more comfortable beginning conversations with folks whom we may or may not know well — but whose beliefs about death we may be totally unaware of. By increasing our understanding about *all* of the beliefs, we will feel more able to be respectful and engaging when we talk about death with others, who may have very different beliefs than we do.

So, let's now discuss each of the Four Belief Systems in greater detail.

Chapter 7

The First Belief System

*"My body dies, and my mind dies.
The life of my mind is connected to
the life of my body."*

The Physical Science View

This was my father's belief system. He was an engineer and had a scientific way of thinking and viewing the world. This belief system is very common among scientists and people who tend to view the world from a very material standpoint, sometimes referred to as "physicalism."

My Parents

Let me step back for a second, and tell you about my parents since they will appear in several of the stories I will tell later in this book.

I'm fairly tall, 6 foot 2 inches, barefoot.

My mother was five feet tall — 5'0", born in China, and emigrated to the United States when she was three years old in 1929. My mom was small in stature, but she was a 'huge' woman in many ways with a big engaging personality. Her name even reflected this. It was "King" — a romanization of how her Chinese name sounded in English.

A Renaissance woman, she was way ahead of her time — a chemist, an abstract artist (the Boston Museum of Fine Arts exhibited her oil paintings in the late 1950's), an incredible gardener (*Better Homes & Gardens* ran a pictorial of her huge backyard rock garden in full bloom in the early 1960's), a seamstress making wedding dresses in our den for the local town aristocracy, a designer and maker of handmade jewelry, and the #1 Fuller Brush salesperson in Massachusetts for over a decade. Mom's success as a Fuller Brush sales manager later paid for my college education.

I outgrew my mom in the fourth grade, and I remember going to a party with her once. I remember it like it was yesterday. It was one of those 'distant relatives-family' parties, where you haven't seen the relatives in decades. A lot of these people hadn't seen my mom since she was a little girl. ... I remember it was a summer, and was held outside in somebody's backyard in suburban Boston, in Westwood, Massachusetts. We arrived a little bit late, so most of the guests were already there — and when we walked in, everybody turned and looked at my mom and then they looked at this tall kid, at me.

I was taller than my mom. Remember — I was only in the fourth grade. And they gasped, "Oh wow, is this your *younger brother*?"

How cool is that, to hear that as a mother?! ... *"Is this your younger brother?"*

My father was also much shorter than I.

So, picture my dad. He was about 5'6", Asian, with a heavy Boston accent, and always had a cigar hanging out of the side of his mouth.

He was a World War II veteran and very proud of it, having served as an officer in the Pacific Theater. He always had his World War II baseball cap on — with an embroidered B-29 bomber on the front.

If you had asked my dad, "What do you think about death, Henry? What's going to happen to you after you die?"

He would often say with some swagger (and out of the side of his mouth since he always had a big cigar stump in his mouth...) —

"Stick me in a box, throw the dirt on me, I'm done."

That's it, just like that. That was my dad. A man of few words.

That's Belief System Number One. A lot of people have that belief about death.

What Happens When We Die?

But let's step back for a second, and think more about this First Belief System.

What happens when we die?

When I say "we" die, what are we talking about?

Remember, in this First Belief System, we are talking about both the physical body *and* the mind dying — because the belief is that the mind is *connected to the life of the body.*

For example, you may have heard some people say —

"The mind is connected to the brain, and when the brain dies, the mind shuts off."

That's another way of articulating this First Belief System.

Okay now, but let's look into this thinking a bit further.

Think about it.

One of two things is going to happen when any of us die, regardless of what our belief system is —

We will either cease to exist,

or

We will continue to exist.

And, as I mentioned earlier, what I mean by "we" is our mind, spirit or consciousness. In other words, when our physical body dies, our mind will either continue to exist or it will not continue to exist.

It's a binary choice. Right? Either one or the other is going to happen when anybody dies.

Now, back to the First Belief System — my dad's

belief system. They believe that the mind shuts off when the body dies. If that's the case, does it make sense to fear death?

First, let's take a look at fear more closely.

Definition of Fear

What is "fear"? I define fear in the following way —

"Fear" is the emotion caused by the anticipation of unhappiness.

Does It Make Sense To Fear Death Within This Belief System?

If that's the case — that fear is the emotion caused by the anticipation of unhappiness — and if my father believes that after his body dies, his mind completely shuts off, then he will have *no experience.* He cannot be happy *or* sad. He will not have any emotion, no mental experience whatsoever.

So, there is no need to fear death now. If you have that First Belief System, then you only have the present life in your physical body. And the focus therefore should be on enjoying life now while you have a physical body and your mind is alive.

And that is exactly how my dad lived his life.

So, you see, by clarifying and increasing our understanding of our belief about death, we can quickly overcome our fear of death if we hold the First Belief System.

Now, some of you may be saying, "Wait a minute! I believe the First Belief System, but I am still afraid of death…"

And you very well may still harbor some fears. But, understand at the outset that those fears you may have are not the fear of death. That would be logically impossible as we have explained above, if in fact you hold this First Belief System.

But…maybe you have a hybrid of the First and Second Belief Systems, like some people do. In that case, you don't solely hold the First Belief System by itself.

For example, you may be afraid of the "nothingness" you anticipate will happen after your body dies. You may call it a "fear of oblivion." You do not want life to end, but you think that it will.

As I have said, if you have this fear, it's good to be clear within yourself that you do *not solely* have the First Belief System. Because a fear based on that would be illogical and impossible as I have discussed above. Instead, you have a hybrid.

You have a hybrid — or a combination — belief. Your belief straddles two of the beliefs that I'm outlining here. You most likely either have a hybrid between the First and Second Beliefs, or a hybrid between the First and Fourth Beliefs.

And I say this most affectionately and with humor — you are a 'straddler.' But, understand that many people are similar to you. Many people straddle two belief systems.

It's completely reasonable to straddle because 'we don't know until we know.' Right? In other words, we won't know what happens when we die, until we die.

So, you may "pretty much" believe in the First Belief System, but you may still have some fears about "what if" you are wrong...

That's okay. Don't be too hard on yourself.

Alternatively, you may be afraid of *related fears* to the fear of death. Many people confuse "the fear of the process of dying" or "the fear of pain and suffering" for the fear of death.

But they are wholly different fears. And as I discussed earlier in this book, the clarification of what our fears are of is very important. It is important so we don't continue living our lives thinking we have more fears than we actually have so we don't waste unnecessary extra energy, and so we can identify the most appropriate solution to overcome those fears. (A detailed discussion of these 'related fears' is covered in my second book.)

Let's discuss the Second Belief System now...

Chapter 8

The Second Belief System

*"My mind continues after my body dies,
and it scares me."*

The Fear of Continued Existence

I refer to this as the "fear of continued existence," because in this belief system the person believes that he or she is continuing — i.e., the mind, soul, or spirit is continuing — *but they're afraid.*

Let's talk about this. What's really going on in that fear?

A number of things are underlying that fear. You have the "fear of the Unknown," not knowing what's going to happen after the body dies and the mind continues — there is uncertainty. You also may be uncertain as to what level of control you will have, in what some people refer to as "the Afterlife."

And more specifically, the uncertainty may be about the fear of going to Heaven or Hell. That fear sometimes terrifies people causing them to feel really unsettled about it — even though they believe that the mind continues after the death of the body.

How Do People Express The "Fear of Continued Existence"?

Sometimes people express this fear in a literal sense. They say, "I am afraid of what is going to happen to me after I die." That is clear.

The challenge is when it is not clear because the person may have confused one or more fears. Here is how that looks...

This happens often when I talk with people about the fear of death — either individually in emails to me, on the phone or in group lectures or workshops. Many people will describe themselves as having the First Belief System.

However, they will say things like, "It is my belief that once I die, I will cease to exist. The thing is I am not at all afraid of the process of dying (although a painless one would be preferable), I am afraid of the concept of non-existence — the 'end' of me as a sentient, living being. It's frightening."

Another person who contacted me said, "The thing that bothers me is that one day, everything I see is going to disappear. I'm kind of indecisive on my belief. Part of me believes in oblivion, which is the one that kind of scares me the most. I understand that you said there's nothing to fear, you won't 'feel' anything. But, I guess what depresses me and scares me is that I'm going to cease to be. I won't be able to experience this world anymore. That would mean I should take advantage of my time here, right? Well, that's my problem. My fear seems to have left me paralyzed. I feel like I have barely any time. I'm only 21. I'm still very young. But I 'feel' as if I'm going to be like 80 in a matter of months or days."

You see the thing is that, as we discussed in the First Belief System, if you really do believe that the brain and the mind are completely dependent on each other, then there will be no existence (of the mind) after the brain (physical body) dies. Yet often, people still harbor a fear, as expressed in these two examples.

So, the first thing I do is "untangle" their thinking. By clarifying that their belief system is not the First Belief System, we can then isolate their fear and state it clearly as the "Fear of Continued Existence," not the fear of non-existence. They quickly see that their fear as they have stated it makes no sense. They are anticipating and fearing an experience of no experience, and that is illogical and impossible.

But while this increased understanding and clarification may lessen their anxiety somewhat, their discomfort still continues, even though it is illogical. So how do we handle and reduce, and even eliminate those vestiges of anxiety?

Overcoming the fear of continued existence requires a second step.

How Can We Completely Handle The "Fear of Continued Existence"?

I suggest that the best way to deal with that fear is in the here and now, so we can prepare ourselves for whatever might happen afterwards.

The solution to overcoming our 'fear of continued existence' is to turn to what I describe here as developing the "ancient Greek sense of virtue" within us.

Ancient Greek Sense Of Virtue

What do I mean by "virtue" in the ancient Greek sense?

It's very important to define this. First let me tell you *what it's not.*

I do not mean virtue in the way *our culture today* often thinks of it — as a set of ethical rules or principles governing conduct. For example, "You've got to do this. Don't do this. Do this and you will be a good person. You should behave this way, then you will be a 'virtuous' person."

Cultures worldwide today typically think of virtue as a set of *behavioral rules.* That's *not* what I'm talking about.

I'm talking about the *ancient Greek sense of virtue* —

Turn within, Know Thyself. Know one's self, and then become a more effective, productive person externally in one's life. If you do that, you can live a happier, more fulfilling life. A virtuous life. That was how they defined a virtuous life.

That was the idea of the ancient Greek sense of virtue — Know Thyself.

Ask yourself, "What makes me tick?" What about *your* personality makes you like this, or see this in a certain way, or hear music in a certain way?

You like certain music. You don't like other music. Explore why that is the case.

Or, let's say you go to a movie. The same people go to the same movie. Yet they have a totally different experience — two different, three different, 20 different people — they walk out with 20 different appreciations of that same movie or 20 different interpretations of certain scenes in that movie.

Why is that?

Because everybody's mind is different. Our personalities are different. How we each view the world is different. The ancient Greeks understood this.

But think about it.

Knowing one's self. What happens if you truly know yourself? Or let's say, if you at least get to know yourself *better*, what happens?

You feel better about yourself, you start to feel more uplifted within yourself, you start to feel more self-confident, more comfortable, your level of self-esteem goes up.

And, in turn, what does that mean?

That means that you feel stronger and you become more effective in your life, so you live a happier life. You get so self-confident that fears start to shed. You start to overcome your fears.

Fears start to drop away.

And with regards to this "fear of continued existence," you start to feel as if after death, the 'continued existence' issue doesn't become as big an issue for you — because no matter what happens, *you feel like you can handle it.*

That's the idea. That's the ancient Greek notion of overcoming fear through increasing virtue.

Turn inside.

It's the 'inside-out' technique. It's the 'go inside first' approach — strengthen yourself — and then on the outside you will feel much better. You can handle things much, much better — more easily, more effectively.

"Conscious of XYZ..."

Let's look at this from another perspective. A more modern Western perspective.

What's another way of looking at this idea of 'turning within'? As I often say, "As compared to what?" So, when we say we need to 'turn within' — turn within as compared to what?

The "Conscious of XYZ..." model is a simple but ingenious model that Charlie, a good friend of mine who is now a philosophy professor, came up with in 1970 when I began teaching meditation.

He said all experience can be captured by the phrase "Conscious of XYZ." The idea is that most people identify themselves with the XYZ's of life — the concrete, easily definable, very specific *objects of experience*. The physical experience of life.

For example, if you go to a party or a reception where you don't know anyone, and someone you meet says, "Tell me about yourself..." — what do you usually say?

I'm guessing that your answer goes something like this, "Well, I'm a doctor (lawyer, student, etc.), and I live in (fill in the blank)."

Then the conversation typically goes to specifics like sports teams, where you went to school, social groups, cars you drive, and maybe even how much money you make. Because this is how many of us define ourselves.

By our things. Stuff we can point to. Stuff we can touch. Material stuff.

But is that all of 'who we are'?

Charlie would point out that we have ignored the left side of the equation, the "Conscious of" side.

Don't we need that part of the equation to even have experience in the first place, to even be able to appreciate the objects of experience? I would say Yes.

And in my terminology, I would call that side "the mind," my mind. I need to have a conscious mind to experience. It is the mental side of experience.

So again, it does not matter where we think or believe that mental experience *comes from*. (I will leave you to debate that point among yourselves.)

But we all can agree that we all have mental experience that is *separate from* our physical experience.

As my friend Charlie would often say, "We are 'conscious of' XYZ, but we are *not* the XYZ's — that is not the totality of our experience." Those external XYZ's are not "who we are."

We are not our cars, we are not our bank accounts, or our clothes, or any of our things. Those things are not our identity — they do not represent what makes us up, they are not what we are made of. If they were, we would disappear if we lost our car. And that is obviously not the case!

We fool ourselves because we associate characteristics of our personality with those things — status with expensive cars, power with money, etc. But even those are "things" in the way that we are discussing. Status and power are fleeting — they come and go. What is constant is our minds.

So, what is the point here?

The point is that this view of looking at our life experience through this "Conscious of XYZ..." model is yet another way to explain the importance of what we mean by "turning within."

Allowing our minds to 'turn within' and experience that conscious side of experience — i.e., our mind experiencing itself — as opposed to always having our experience immersed in the things of the world, provides us with balance in life. It gives us inner stability which breeds self-confidence.

And that is the key to overcoming the "Fear of Continued Existence," or any other fear for that matter.

Jimmy Still Wondered...

This story will shed further light on both the First Belief System and the Second Belief System, as well as the idea of "turning within." Remember how I said we can have "hybrid" belief systems, or be "straddlers"? My friend Jimmy was one.

Jimmy was bedridden, could not walk easily, but was still lucid and talking. He ate and drank liquids, but sparingly. He was not yet at the end stages of the dying process, but he was approaching it.

I sat with him one morning last August, about a month before he actually passed away. And after I taught him to meditate, we talked for a few minutes about death. [Caveat: that's not my normal mode in meditation classes, but given the severity of Jimmy's illness and decline, I thought I should take the opportunity to talk with him when I had the chance.]

I asked him what he thought happened after we die. He said he thought, "That was it. Nothing. When we're done, we're done." I said, "That's what my father believed too." Jimmy was describing what I now call the First Belief System.

But then Jimmy said, "But I still wonder."

I asked him, "You wonder about what?" I didn't want to put words or my thoughts into his mind, so I just asked him questions to help me clarify what he was saying, what he meant.

He said, "I wonder if that's what will happen — if I will actually just die. Or if something else will happen."

"Like what?" I asked. "I dunno, like maybe I might not die," he responded.

"Oh. So you think your mind is probably going to stop when you die, but you wonder what may happen if it doesn't?" He said, "Yeah."

So, I held his hand. I wanted him to feel my touch as I talked with him, so he just wasn't "in his head" thinking about this. I wanted him to feel my lack of fear about death, that whatever happened to us, I was okay with it. But, I didn't want to just tell him that, because that just doesn't work, in my experience. He needed to experience it himself, the lack of fear, within himself directly.

So, we talked some more…with me holding the hand of this 6'4", 275 pound former Cobra Attack gunship helicopter pilot. A tough Vietnam War vet and U.S. Army lifer.

Jimmy said, "Yeah, I still wonder about it sometimes. But I'm not afraid of it."

At this point, I kind of did a scan of how I thought he felt…not always 100% accurate, but I do that to just check and after all these years, I'm usually pretty right on…and, he didn't feel afraid to me. But I've seen and heard this hesitation before, and it often means the person may have just a little bit of fear they are harboring — understandably so, because nobody really knows for sure until death actually happens. As I often say, "We don't know 'til we know."

So, I said to Jimmy, "Well, just in case your mind continues after you die, let's talk about what may happen." And I didn't talk with him long about it. I didn't want it to sound to him like I was lecturing. I just told him a short story about a friend of mine from college who had an NDE, a near-death experience. I told him what had happened to my friend (which you will read later in this book), and I said, "I don't know if that's what will happen to you when you die, but that's just food for thought."

Jimmy said, "Well that's an interesting story, pretty wild stuff." And his hand seemed to relax just slightly in mine.

Then I changed subjects and asked him to tell me about being in the Army when he was stationed in Germany after Vietnam. And his face lit up, and his hand definitely relaxed in mine even more…

Jimmy died a month later. I was fortunate to be by his bedside at that moment he passed — standing alongside his wife Donna and his daughter Kim. He died peacefully.

So, in retrospect, Jimmy may have been one of those rare multi-hybrids. He said he believed in the First Belief System, and lived his life fully, seemingly without fear, or not much. But maybe he had a little fear of continued existence, the Second Belief System. Or, maybe he was even of the Third Belief System and didn't even really know it, wasn't consciously aware that he was. But in the end, he died calmly, sharing some final words with me a few days before he passed, and my fear radar tells me that he died pretty much fear-free.

Chapter 9

The Third Belief System

"My body dies, my mind continues.
It transitions to something.
I'm not sure to what, but it doesn't scare me."

How It Is Described

In this belief system, they believe that the mind does not cease to exist after the physical body dies. Instead, the mind continues on — after the body dies and turns to dust.

This belief system is similar to the Second Belief System with one key distinguishing feature — there is *no fear of continued existence.*

For any number of reasons, the person does not have a fear of what may happen after they physically die. This may be attributed to any of the following (or a combination thereof) — strong inner sense of self, a connection with oneself internally, self-confidence, experience related to having almost physically died but then having come back into the body (an NDE), or strong religious or spiritual beliefs that one will be taken care of after one dies physically.

Plus, this belief system includes the idea that after the person dies, their mind continues and *transitions* to some other place that is different from living on the physical planet Earth. It is a place that is non-physical in the usual sense of the word "physical." Personalities (or minds) do not have physical bodies that they need to feed and sustain — there is no need to eat — so the usual daily stresses we have on Earth in physical bodies do not exist there.

There is a feeling of being at peace. One can move about more freely than on Earth, more easily, more quickly. And it is like being on vacation.

Different cultures and religions through different eras in history have called this 'place' various names. For example, it has been referred to as Heaven, Nirvana, Afterlife, Paradise, Zion, Valhalla, Spirit World, and Elysium.

Some believe that the individual mind can stay there forever, or for as long as it wishes. Others believe that the mind must leave at certain times and under certain conditions. I will leave the details of that to your own further research, as there is a great deal that has already been written about the various cultural and religious views on the entrance and exit — the going to and from — this place, whatever we may call it.

But our focus here is on helping us overcome our fear of death.

Perhaps some of the following stories and experiences may help those who find themselves in the Second Belief System feel more comfortable with the "continued existence" they believe in. Maybe it will help them reduce their fears somewhat and move closer to the Third Belief System.

So, let's look into this idea of the mind possibly continuing after the body dies in a bit more detail with that objective in mind.

"Near-Death Experiences"

Have you or anybody you know ever had a "Near-Death Experience"? It is also commonly known by the acronym "NDE."

NDE's are experiences that an individual has that is associated with impending death, which can encompass any combination of multiple possible sensations including mental detachment from the body, feelings of levitation or lightness, being at peace or total serenity, feeling safe or secure, warmth, and the presence of light.

According to a Gallup Poll conducted in 1992, 13 million Americans reported having had an NDE. At that time, that was 5% of the U.S. population. Similar statistical studies have been conducted in other countries with similar results.

For those of you who don't know what this is or haven't had the experience — a Near-Death Experience — I'll describe a couple of them to you.

Henry's Tonsils

A friend of mine in college had an NDE. He told me about it when we were in college, but it happened to him when he was eight years old.

He had his tonsils out. Many of you probably know people who have had their tonsils removed. It's a fairly common surgical procedure, right?

After he had his tonsils out, he came home and his mom felt badly for him. So what did she do? She gave him a cookie. Not a good idea. He ate the cookie, and it promptly severed all the sutures. Henry told me that at this point, he "was vomiting up balls of blood."

Here's where my friend's NDE starts...

He said "he" (i.e., his mind) was up on the ceiling looking down at his eight-year-old body and it was not in good shape, he saw himself passed out, vomiting blood — *not* good things happening — and he saw his mom who was really upset.

Henry told me, "My mother called the doctor. When the doctor finally arrived, he freaked out because he saw I had lost a huge amount of blood and I was fading away. He immediately put me in his car and drove me to the hospital because he didn't want to wait for an ambulance."

Henry, whose body (and mind) appeared unconscious to external observers, 'saw' the whole thing. He said he heard and remembered all the conversations that went on, all of that. And throughout the entire experience, he felt very peaceful, he felt completely calm inside, and had no fear.

He said, "I remember looking at my poor mother who looked so worried, and I was feeling very expanded and peaceful. So, I told her not to worry."

Then, he came back into his body. He obviously lived — otherwise he wouldn't have been telling me this story or been my roommate in graduate school! He recently told me that as a result of that NDE, he has never had a fear of death.

Now, I am *not* suggesting that we all run out and try to have NDE's ourselves, but I am suggesting that these numerous medically-documented experiences may be strong indicators to support those who believe this Third Belief System — that the mind may continue after the physical body dies, and that one can experience that without fear.

That was my college friend's experience of his particular Near-Death Experience. However, there are many different variations of NDE's.

Here's another one…

Jay in the ER

Another friend of mine, Jay, was medically dead for 20 minutes — a very long time.

He had been in the hospital emergency room that night, but then was moved to another room in the morning. Our friend Diane had been with him throughout the night and accompanied him to the new room.

She told me, "He 'coded' right in front of me and I went to get help after hitting the button, and told the nurses he was not breathing — they quickly came in and checked him, and then they yelled *'Code!'* And then about 10 people rushed in — doctors and nurses."

"Coded" is medical slang meaning that a patient is having a cardiopulmonary arrest (the heart has stopped beating) in a hospital or clinic, requiring a team of providers to rush to the specific location and begin immediate efforts to try to resuscitate him, to bring his body back to life — the 'paddles on the chest' routine that you see on TV and in the movies.

Keep in mind, the National Institute of Health states that, "Permanent brain damage begins after only 4 minutes without oxygen, and death can occur as soon as 4 to 6 minutes later."

And, for the most part, that's true for almost everyone in the world. Except for my friend Jay.

This is what he and Diane (who was in the hospital room sitting with Jay at his bedside during this entire NDE) described to me...

Diane was praying for Jay, and did what she called "petitioning for him" — asking for his life to continue and for advice. She said, "I was 'told' to sing three pujas and ignore all that was going on, to not speak to anyone as I was shown in advance the entire scene and that he would live.

"A Presence came over me as I sang softly and I focused 100% on the puja and Jay," Diane said.

(She was singing a familiar song they both knew — called the "puja" — which Diane had been singing for many years and Jay would have recognized.)

In 2014, Jay described his NDE to me in detail. The event happened in 2004.

Here is what Jay told me —

He said "he" left the hospital room — i.e., his "mind" — his mind left his body, and then he found himself in what he described as "a crystalline, dense star field — like out in outer space." He said he then "started to move through it, and then past it."

Jay said, contrary to what some people describe in their NDE's, he "did not go down a 'tunnel' — not at first." He said he experienced "a void, a blackness, and silence." He also said he "knew if [he] went further, [he] would not have come back." He said he had a choice to continue further or not.

At that point in his NDE, Jay "heard a lilting song, a melody." He didn't recognize the song, but he found it pleasant, "warm and comforting."

As I mentioned, Diane, who was standing right next to Jay's bed at that moment in the hospital room, was singing to him a familiar song they both knew — called the puja.

And then, Jay told me, "I felt myself being drawn back."

At that point, Jay found himself "in a tunnel going really fast." He had a sense of speed because "…along the sides of the tunnel were robed figures, though not in bodies in the usual way we see people on Earth."

Then he went faster and faster down the tunnel towards the pleasant, lilting song. Unbeknownst to Jay, his mind was moving towards his friend Diane.

Remember, as I said, Diane was singing — standing at Jay's bedside. And then she saw the doctors on each side of the bed stop what they had been doing.

And she heard the doctors say, "Let us synchronize our watches…" — as they were preparing to call out his official time of death.

A minister had come in and wanted to comfort Diane. Diane told her to let her be, that she (Diane) was also a minister — and Diane told her, "He is going to live" — saying it with authority to the room in general. Then Diane went silent.

At that point, Diane heard someone on 'the other side' tell her, "Speak briefly with authority," and so Diane said, in a strong voice, "His hand moved…." The doctors and nurses all looked very surprised at her and they quickly intubated Jay again, starting the series of resuscitation procedures — all over again.

Remember, 20 minutes had now transpired since he had 'coded.'

Then, Jay described it to me like this — he said, "Kel, then I felt like I *slammed* into my body."

He 'came down' so fast, it was as if his mind felt like it slammed into his body incredibly fast. And when it did, he sat bolt upright, and scared the heck out of the doctors and the nurses! Everybody was totally freaked out, because they all thought he had been dead for 20 minutes.

And when Jay sat right up, he started yelling, really pissed off looking around the hospital room, "Diane, where am I? Who are *these people*!?"

He then described the NDE experience to Diane, adding that he also saw "a tall Presence standing behind [her] with hands outstretched." Jay drew a sketch of this for Diane, including the Presence behind her, and of the gold light that was emanating from that Presence.

Diane said that what was so amazing was that Jay was immediately filled with life, and every time someone came in to the hospital room, he told them what had happened. He also no longer had any allergies! (They disappeared after that NDE.) They then moved him to a room down the hall and very shortly thereafter sent him home.

His family doctor was surprised saying that "diabetics do not usually come back" — Jay had been diabetic since age 11 and had had many hospitalizations with various complications over the years. Jay was 51 years old at the time of his NDE.

So, that's another Near-Death Experience — a very different NDE from my college friend's experience. As you can see, there is a wide range of these experiences.

Why Am I Discussing NDE's?

Because it's another 'data point' to consider as we contemplate death and dying.

There are tens of thousands of these reported NDE cases that have been witnessed by doctors and nurses worldwide. Many have been medically documented — at least insofar as they occurred while the patient was fully connected to and being measured by the usual battery of medical devices and instruments while they were undergoing surgery or some other reason for their hospitalization.

And in studies done by various organizations including the Gallup Poll, millions of other people worldwide report having them each year.

So, it's another 'data point' that may help us think more about the *possibility* of 'life' continuing after the death of the body. And, not in a fearful way — but instead, in what is generally reported as a peaceful way.

Is it proof that there's "life after death"?

I don't think these reports — regardless of how many there regularly are each year or how common their structure seems to be — are necessarily proof, but they certainly raise questions in people's minds. And that's what I'm doing.

I would also like to see bona fide scientific research conducted on NDE's. And by "bona fide" I mean truly objective research — because not all studies are. I would like to see studies done that are unbiased — that don't merely start out trying to debunk the idea of NDE's, nor to confirm their reality. No fake science. And that means studies that are funded by entities that have no 'skin in the game' other than finding out 'what is what.' No vested interest in the outcome other than science and knowledge.

If you look for studies on NDE's, there is a dearth of them. And the camps that exist around NDE's are extreme — the believers who refer to themselves as "experiencers" and the non-believers who call the experiencers quacks and charlatans. Name calling is not very productive. And it certainly does not advance scientific thought or knowledge.

More bold scientists need to take this task on. I think the results could be eye-opening, if done honestly and thoroughly.

Again, I'm not discussing NDE's to encourage you to believe this way or that way. I want to encourage people to think on their own. To consider the various data that is available, then draw one's own conclusions and perspectives.

And as I mentioned, while there is a huge range of different kinds of experiences that can happen in any given NDE, there is also a similarity that occurs across *all* NDE's — where it seems that the mind is continuing long after the person is supposed to be *physically dead*, and then they 'come back' into their body. And that's of course how we know about it.

My point is just to raise these experiences and cause us to think, "Hmmm, maybe let's think more about this."

Ask ourselves what these experiences may mean in terms of death — in terms of the "death of the mind."

It is what I like to call another data point to consider, as we contemplate our respective beliefs about death.

Perhaps it will prompt us to ask ourselves, "If so many people worldwide — across all religions and cultures — have had documented NDE experiences like these, how does that impact our (my) thinking in our (my) respective belief systems?"

My Father and the Road to Waikiki

Continuing our discussion about the Third Belief System, let's talk about my father again.

He knew he was dying for about a year before he died — the colon cancer had come back within two years of his treatment and surgery, so he knew he was nearing the end of his road. He asked me to take care of everything — 'line up all the ducks,' make sure all of his papers were in order, contact the long list of people in his friends and family network at the designated time — and so I did.

Growing up with my dad was difficult.

He was a tough guy to feel close to. Like many men of his generation, he was not emotive at all — he basically had two gears — funny and angry. Not a lot in between — not if you were one of his kids, and certainly not the eldest son.

Mostly he was emotionally neutral, all business. In fact, he once told me that he only cried twice in his entire life — once at age 16 when his 18-year-old brother died of appendicitis, and once when my mom died. That was it.

And the last thing he ever showed was love. I honestly don't recall ever getting a hug from him, just a few handshakes congratulating me when I received the next rank on my way to Eagle Scout, and when I graduated from college, and later law school — that sort of thing.

But in a crisis — like when I got in a 60 MPH car accident on the highway with my high school girlfriend on our way to see "Romeo & Juliet" — he was totally present and supportive emotionally, telling me when he arrived on the scene after the police had left that, "It was all right…", that "Everything would be fine." And that the guy in the Ford Falcon who had caused the accident and driven off into the dark winter night on Route 128 would have to live with knowing what he had done.

Except for that type of rare situation, my dad and I knocked heads throughout my teens. Then, at age 19, while I was away at college I learned how to meditate, how to 'turn within,' got myself centered inside, and realized I would never be able to change him. And so I relaxed in our relationship and let him be who he was.

By now — three decades after I had learned to meditate — I also had the benefit of a lot more life experience. So unlike when my mom died almost twenty years earlier, now that my dad was ready to leave the Earth, I was ready to be there for him — fully. To support his exit in whatever way he wanted.

Remember — he was a World War II veteran.

He had tried several times to qualify as a fighter pilot, and even memorized the details of how to fly a plane from books he had read. However, he flunked the eyesight test twice, and the next time when he had memorized the eye chart, he weighed in under the minimum weight for his height! The next time he went back, he ate a huge breakfast and four extra bananas prior to the weigh-in, but he was still supposedly underweight.

I always questioned his decision to eat four extra bananas…really?…how much weight are bananas going to add…but, I never said anything to him! I also never mentioned my thoughts about whether he was being discriminated against since he was Asian, and the Japanese had just bombed Pearl Harbor, and the U.S. government was in the process of rounding up all Japanese-Americans and locking them up in internment camps…I never said anything to my dad because he was so proud to have been an American fighting for the United States in the Pacific.

So, after a short stint as an engineering officer with a B-24 group in Clovis, New Mexico, he shipped out on the USS Mount Vernon, a troop transfer ship (before the war it had been a luxury ocean liner, the SS Washington) which transported him to his Pacific Theater assignment. My kids still have a dollar bill my dad gave them on which he wrote the name of the ship, his name and dog tag number, along with the signatures of four of his buddies who were with him — all signed "Lt." (Lieutenant). All five of them were young officers in their early 20's, all Second Lieutenants.

My dad spent most of World War II supervising the maintenance of the B-29's of the 444th Bomb Group in the U.S. Army Air Corps and later the U.S. Army Air Forces (USAAF), the predecessors to the U.S. Air Force (USAF). He was stationed in India (flying "the Hump" — over the Himalayas), and later in Kwanghan, China.

He was so proud of having served his country in the 1940's as a World War II vet, that he went to every reunion of his bomb group, originally about 2,000 men. He even served as an officer of the reunion committee a number of times.

So, it was no surprise to me that he wanted to be buried in the U.S. military cemetery in Hawaii.

It is a beautiful cemetery. And if you have never visited it, you should. It is in the crater of an extinct volcano. Thus, the locals call it the "Punch Bowl" — with a panoramic view overlooking Waikiki Beach and

Diamond Head in the distance. The view is absolutely stunning.

The official name is the "National Memorial Cemetery of the Pacific." My father's last wishes were very clear and specific. He wanted to be cremated and have his ashes interred there at the columbarium with full military honors as a Captain in the United States Air Force — Captain Henry W.F. Chin, USAF.

So, I made all the arrangements, submitting all the proof of military service and honorable discharge paperwork with the U.S. military authorities, and we took his ashes there from Los Angeles.

Experience in the Hotel on Waikiki

About three months after he died, in the Spring of 1999 my siblings and our families all convened in Hawaii for my dad's funeral services at the military cemetery. And since we had many young children at the time and we were flying in from different time zones, I suggested that we all meet at the Moana Surfrider Hotel's beach because it's an iconic, beautiful Hawaiian hotel built in 1901 (Waikiki's first hotel) with an awesome beach…and as those of you who have had children know, the beach is always a great, free babysitter!

So that evening, after everyone arrived, to keep it simple I suggested we all just go eat at the Chinese restaurant in the lobby of our hotel, across the street at the Sheraton Princess Kaiulani Hotel.

And since our daughter Sammie was 5 years old and we wanted to get her to bed as soon as dinner was over, I sent everyone else off to order the food while I took her upstairs to rinse her off, and get her into her pajamas. So, we did that, came back downstairs, and two hours later we were all done with dinner.

My sister Lorinda is the one in the family with no children, so she's the best aunt on the planet. "Oh, I'll take the kids to the gift shop!" she said (in true form) after dinner.

At this point in the evening it's about 10:00 PM, so I said, "That's great, but I'm going to take Sammie and put her to bed." So she and I went upstairs.

And, here's what we saw…

First of all, those of you who know me, know that I travel a lot. I have always traveled a lot — for decades — for work. As a result, I have developed a habit of being very, very careful about hotel doors and making sure that they are shut completely. I jiggle the handle, asking myself, "Did it click?" All of that. I even do it quietly but firmly, so I'm not waking up all the neighbors. I close it, I listen for the "Click"…then I go.

I'm that guy.

So, here is what Sammie and I saw when we returned to the room —

The door to the hotel room was *completely wide open*, and on all of the hotel room doors at the Sheraton

Princess Kaiulani Hotel were these magnetic door stops where you could open the door all the way — and magnetize it, holding the door wide open. I think it may have been for the maids or the bellmen, or for yourself getting your luggage in more easily. So, you could easily just open the door all the way, and have it automatically magnetize and stay open.

That's how we found the door when we got back upstairs to the hotel room.

The room was pitch black.

Remember, there were four of us — four suitcases — and it was not a big room. So the suitcases were spread out all over the floor. And, my suitcase was the one closest to the door, right there when you open the door. Sitting right on top of it was my scuba-diving regulator. It was still there, untouched.

Nothing was touched in the room.

I called down to the front desk. And I said, "Geez, I think somebody may have broken into our room. I don't know. But, I don't see anything missing."

They proceed to send two security guys up, two Hawaiian security guys. They plug in their keyboard to the door lock and, with the computer software in the actual keyboard itself, can tell whose key was the last key that opened the door — and exactly at what time.

It was my key at 7:40 PM when I brought Sammie up to rinse her off and put her in her jammies.

So at this point, these two security guys are scratching their heads and saying, "We can't figure it out, Mr. Chin. It was your key. We have no explanation for this." Then I said, "This is really weird." And I added, "This is really weird, man. We're all here. Our families are here — we're all going up to the Punch Bowl tomorrow to take my dad's ashes up there for his ceremony."

Then, these two Hawaiian guys looked at me like this…they did a 'double take.' And as if it were scripted from a *Saturday Night Live* skit, they both — at the same time — looked at me with this look on their faces, as if saying, "What are you, duh-h-h-m-b…?" But then they both — again at the same time — this time in chorus and with energy and emphasis, said, "That was your dad! He's *messing* with you!"

You see, native Hawaiians believe in "spirit," that the mind continues after the body dies. So to them, it was a no-brainer.

That was the first thing that happened.

The *second thing* happened when we woke up the next morning…

At this point we were going to go have breakfast before the 10:30 military service up at the Punch Bowl. So, I went to the safe and entered the four-digit code to get my wallet out to go to breakfast. Then I locked the door again to the safe, because we had airplane tickets and travelers checks safely stowed away in there.

Two seconds later I gasped, "Ah! That's right!" …I had forgotten to take out the four coupons for our last meal at the hotel. And since we were going to stay on a different island right after the funeral service for the rest of the trip, breakfast was the last meal where we would be able to use the coupons at this hotel for the free meal.

However, when I went to punch the key code in again, the screen on the safe was blank. So I said to our son Jesse, who was 10 years old then, "Jess, maybe the power's out in the whole hotel. Check the bathroom…" (the bathroom light worked) "Check the light at the nightstand between the beds." (it worked) Okay, it wasn't the whole hotel, so I tried to turn the TV on… (it didn't work).

Now, because of what happened the night before, I was a little suspicious — maybe curious is a better word — or, maybe I was a little of both. So I just carefully looked over onto the other side of that big piece of furniture — the TV stand and dresser combo — and I looked at the power strip that the TV, refrigerator and safe were all plugged into.

And you know how power strips have an on/off button, a *red* on/off button? A button you can push in either direction?

Well, because of what happened the night before, I just took a moment and looked at it carefully first — without touching it. I just looked at that red on/ off button, and studied it closely, because I thought maybe it was a loose connection. Maybe the button was pushed halfway down or something.

No such luck.

It was pushed *all the way off*. The red light was off — that side of the button was completely pushed down.

I thought, "Okay, this is weird." I turned it back on. I punched the 4-digit code into the safe, and got the four 'free meal' coupons.

That was the second thing that happened.

Here's the *third thing* that happened...

Now at this point in the story we're downstairs having breakfast. Then after we finished, even though I had the four meal coupons, I always tip on the full value of the meal. So when our young waiter came back to our table — there were about 20 waitpersons in that big Waikiki restaurant — I gave him his tip and looked at his name tag... He had the *same name* as my father — *Henry* — this Asian kid who's like 17, 18 years old is named "Henry."

Not a very common name at the time for 17-year-old Asians in Hawaii.

He walked away and I turned to the family and said, "Did you guys see that kid's name tag?" And Jesse said, "Yeah Dad, I saw it when we first sat down, but with all this stuff that's been going on, it was just way too weird...so I didn't say anything!"

Who knows? Was it my father sending us messages from the 'other side'? I don't know. Who knows? I'm not saying it necessarily was, but it's another data point, another question mark.

Maybe it was...

Because that would have been completely consistent with his personality — he was very detail-oriented, very controlling. He had to have everything very much done 'his way.' All the "t's" crossed and all the "i's" dotted. And I am sure he wanted to make sure the ceremony was done exactly right — the full 21-gun salute by the riflemen, the tightly folded American flag — everything done exactly as promised. Full military honors.

He knew that I would take care of it, but he was watching, I think.

Maybe.

Who knows?

In retrospect, I actually think my dad may have been a little surprised after he died…surprised that he 'continued.'

Visits from Dead Relatives or Friends

So, while the story about what may have been my dad sending messages from the 'other side' is factually accurate (since all of us in the family observed the three situations I just described), it is still conjecture regarding whether it was actually him trying to communicate with us.

However, there are many instances reported by people around the world who claim to have been actually *visited* by dead relatives or friends. They report that this happens in their dreams, in their meditations, and even while they are wide awake.

Sometimes they see them, or something that looks like them (some describe it as "a light body" or "an energy form"). Other times they hear them, or smell their unique body scent or perfume, or hear some music that is unique to them. It can come in many forms.

But in each case, the people often feel certain that what they experienced was real.

Here are a few examples…

A High School Classmate

Twenty years ago a close friend of mine from college was living in Muenster, Germany, and he woke up at 3:30 early on a December morning from a lucid dream ("lucid" meaning that he was awake inside and fully aware of what was happening…not like those dreams where we are sort of 'out of it' and elephants can turn into flowers, and that sort of thing).

In the dream, he was standing outside the side entrance to his high school, and the door opened. One of his classmates, who had had a severely debilitating form of multiple sclerosis for over a decade, was standing in the doorway, but was afraid of coming out. So, she asked my friend to deliver a message to her younger sister.

"Please tell her I am fine. She is worried about me, but she doesn't need to be."

My friend, in the dream, looked to the side and could see his classmate's younger sister standing on the lawn in front of the school's main entrance. She was standing behind a table and was talking to about 8 people who were sitting in chairs facing her.

My friend then turned back to his classmate, who smiled shyly and disappeared back inside the school.

Then my friend woke up.

It was immediately clear to my friend that that lucid dream had been a real request from his classmate, who had been one of his neighborhood friends since kindergarten, and that the dream imagery and message indicated that she had recently died. So he contacted the younger sister and found out that his classmate had indeed passed away a few days earlier, and that the younger sister had been worried about her sister because her MS had been so severe that she had not been able to communicate with her family for years.

The younger sister also told my friend that at the time he woke up from the lucid dream she had been giving a talk at her family's company Christmas party, and that she had been standing behind a table with about 8 employees sitting in chairs in front of her. Right at 8:30 pm — the time it was in Wisconsin when my friend woke up 4,000 miles away.

Although my friend knew about his classmate's serious illness, he had no idea previous to this experience that his classmate had died until she 'visited him' in Germany. He had not been in contact with her since high school — over 20 years earlier — nor did he know the whereabouts of her sister or anything about their relationship with each other.

No Smoking in Heaven

This happened to me in January 2015. Early in the morning at 6:10 AM, I was woken up by someone's energy. You know how you can sometimes feel someone standing or sitting near you, but you don't look over at them yet? Then you look, and sure enough, there they are?

It was like that. Except there was no one I could see there. It was just the feeling that there was someone there near me.

I could tell it was a "he." I don't know how I knew that, I just knew it. And he told me he was Nancy's brother. Nancy is a friend of mine in Phoenix. I knew that she had had a brother who had died, but I didn't know any more than that.

He told me to tell her various messages, including that he was doing fine and that he had tried to get a message to her but that it wasn't that easy. Since the other parts of the messages are personal between the two of them regarding their relationship, I won't share them here. The content of that part of the messages is not important to our discussion here, and I always honor people's privacy.

What is interesting and not of such a sensitive nature, is that he mentioned two very odd things — at least I thought they were odd and somewhat out of place at the time. He mentioned that there is no smoking where he is, and at the end of our conversation, he 'showed' me a visual of Nancy and him going out at night to a nightclub that he said was in San Diego.

When I told Nancy those two odd parts of the message, it immediately made sense to her.

She told me he absolutely hated cigarette smoke (of which I had no previous knowledge), and that a week before he died, they both went to a nightclub in San Diego together where he sang karaoke and got a standing ovation from the crowd! That was the last time she saw him — 16 years earlier.

So, by telling me to tell her those two specific (what I thought were totally random) parts of the message, I think her brother may have been trying to give her a personal message within the message to let her know that it, in fact, was he who was sending her this message.

Later, Nancy told me that her brother Mitchell had committed suicide. So, for her it carried an extra level of pain. Suicide is a special kind of pain for the survivors. It's very hard to reconcile. Many people believe that God condemns people who commit suicide to hell. But certainly any loving God would not condemn those who are so upset, at one moment, that they take their own lives.

Nancy told me —

"My brother's message to me proved that. He is not in some place known as hell. His message ended my 16 years of agony. Last year on November 10th is the first time I didn't cry. I acknowledged him with love and I didn't fall apart.

"Kel, I didn't tell you that in his suicide note to me he said that he would try to get a message to me somehow. And in his message to you he said that it wasn't that easy. But at last he was able to and finally I got the relief that I so desperately needed to move forward. I just needed to know that he was okay. He was all alone when he died and that also broke my heart.

"The Heidorn Lifeline, a suicide and crisis hotline specializing in LGBTQ-related challenges, still operates in San Diego County in the LGBT community (originally under the San Diego LGBT Community Center, and now through the San Diego Center for Children). It's a comfort to me to know that my brother lives on through this endowment created in his name by his partner. Through his death he is now helping others to deal with the issues that he struggled with and which ultimately led to his own suicide."

Christmas Gifts

Pam is one of those people who remembers her dreams. Not everyone does. But she does. She was also very close with her mom.

Pam told me that about 6-8 months after her mom died, she had a dream — a very clear, vivid dream. In this dream, Pam had bought her mom a lot of gifts since it was Christmas time (it was not actually Christmas season in Pam's 'waking state' world, just in this dream). In the dream, her phone rang. She looked at the Caller ID and it showed that it was her mom calling, and when Pam answered the phone, it was her mom's voice. Unmistakably her voice.

Pam said, "Oh my God! Where are you?! I have all these gifts for you. Come back!"

Her mom said, "Please don't make me come back. It's beautiful here. It's wonderful here. And I'm so happy here! What am I going to do with all those gifts here? You're just going to have to use them, Pam!"

At that point, Pam said she woke up suddenly, sat up in bed, and asked herself, "Did I just dream that?" Because it felt so real. And...Pam could *smell* her mom's perfume in the bedroom! Her mom always wore a lot of perfume, and it got on her clothes, everywhere, all the time.

In retrospect, Pam thinks her mom was letting her know she was all right, that she was happy where she was. And that the "gifts she should keep and use" represented her mom telling her that Pam could do it without her, that she could live life without her mom, that Pam would be okay. That her mom had taught her how to survive and be fine — those were the 'gifts' her mom told her to use for herself.

Jon's Brother

My friend Jon and I used to work in a law firm together several years ago. When he heard I was writing this book, he recently told me this story that happened to him when he was 23 years old. Jon said he thought it might help others with their concerns about death and dying, and losing a loved one.

His brother died suddenly in a car accident when he was 18 years old. The accident was devastating to the family but especially to their mother, who wanted to see her youngest son again. Deaths like this one are especially difficult because the person is in your life one minute, and gone from your life in the next minute. Sudden and immediate.

About three months after that, Jon had a dream —

"In the dream, I had a conversation with my brother. It was a nice conversation and we laughed. He was perfect, however, no sign of injury. I do not remember much of what was said, but I remember that he said he would have come sooner but he had been busy. I asked him to visit our mother. He said he would. I did not tell my mother that I had that dream.

"However, two days later, I got a call from her saying that my brother had visited her in a dream. My mother enjoyed having a conversation with him. He said to her he would have visited sooner but he was climbing a mountain with a friend. I never dreamed of him again."

These two experiences helped both Jon and his mother to feel at peace with the sudden loss of their brother and son.

Jon also told me, "I remember it as if it was just matter of fact. Sort of like a call from a brother whom you loved and a chance to say goodbye, but nothing more than that. When I woke up right afterwards, I was just happy that it happened and that he seemed happy. I do not question its validity because that would serve no purpose. I guess, I am saying, some things we should just take at face value and count them as blessings and not look much further beyond that."

Caller ID

Someone recently told me that her father died, and a few months after his passing, she got a series of three separate phone calls, days apart. Each time she looked at her phone's Caller ID and each time her father's name and number appeared on her screen. And each time there was total silence on the other end of the line.

Each time she would ask, "Dad, is that you? ... Dad?"

Silence.

The interesting thing is that she had her father's phone disconnected immediately — within days after he died. And he only had a 'land line,' no cell phone. His old fashioned, corded land line phone was sitting in her closet in a box, unplugged and disconnected.

So, each time this happened she was receiving a call — at least if you go by what her Caller ID screen was telling you — from her father's *disconnected* land line. How could that be possible?

Is it possible that someone else got his phone number after he died? Yes, that is totally possible. But how would that person know her phone number to call? It would not be from hitting "Redial" on the phone, because the phone was in a box in her closet. And, how could the Caller ID appear as her father's name and number?

Very odd to say the least. Was it her father trying to reach out to her and contact her? Who knows, but it certainly makes you wonder.

Diane's Dad

My friend Diane had a lucid dream in 1982. I am going to give you a short summary of it here, but if you would like to read the entire, very detailed account of her dream, I have included it in Appendix III at the end of this book.

In her dream, Diane was in the living room of the old house where she had grown up with her family in West Seattle, Washington. She heard a noise in the kitchen, walked over to see who was in the house, and found herself looking at her dad. She ran up to him and they hugged happily, and he asked her if she wanted a toasted cheese sandwich. Diane then said, "Don't you know what happened to you and where you are?"

He smiled and said, "Yes, do you?"

She replied, "You mean that you know you physically died?"

He said, "Yes, but I didn't want to shock you, I didn't know how it would be for us...it took me a while... dying wasn't anything like I ever thought or heard of. I'm not dead and it's like a dream for me that I was there on Earth or even sick....." He then described in detail what he experienced 2-1/2 months earlier while he was dying, sick in the hospital, but not physically dead yet.

Later in this dream, Diane asked her dad what dying felt like and if he felt scared.

He said, "No, it's like falling asleep and dreaming... on the last day in the hospital while I was half asleep, I heard Mama tell me that it was 'Ok to let go.' So I just let go and then woke up immediately at the other place."

He then described to Diane the other place he woke up in, what it looked like, who was there to greet him, and other details.

Then he looked at Diane, seemingly noticing something and asked, "You have been unhappy, haven't you?" Diane answered that she had been, and was not ready for him to leave, and that she missed him very much. Evidently, he had just retired 6 months before he passed away from cancer. Diane was 30 years old at the time.

Diane asked him if he felt lonely or missed her mother, or any friends or relatives still on Earth. And if he had seen any of his friends, family members or others he had known who had passed away before he had. He said that he "...never felt lonely because [he] always feels us and those [he] loves," that he "felt at peace, because we are always connected in the heart, the soul, and that this is true for everyone with deep relationships." He also said he "would not see any of the people in his life who did not love him, only those with whom he had good relationships and friendships, where there was mutual love and caring, and only good memories and experiences are remembered."

He told Diane that she "could talk to him anytime and that when she did, he "will feel and hear [her] and to tell this to Mama, for it would help her as well as others whom [Diane] shared this experience with."

He added that, "Being with them [people who are dying] and giving love is critical while they are passing, as well as having the room being quiet…helping the atmosphere and their feelings to be at peace."

After hearing more details about his experience on 'the other side,' Diane said she felt relieved and felt tears on her face. That she was grateful to have this experience and to hear how happy he was, and that even waiting for her mother did not bother him at all, because he felt her all the time, even if she did not realize it.

At this point in the lucid dream, Diane started to feel a tugging sensation in her body and knew that she was going to have to leave the dream soon. At that point, her daddy hugged her again and said, "Now don't forget to tell Mama what we talked about!" She looked at him and said, "I won't, daddy!"

Diane gently returned to her sleeping body, and immediately got up and wrote down her experience.

Lights Going On in the Car

Donna's husband of 46 years died in September 2015. Jimmy had been sick with cancer for eight years. So while his passing was not a surprise, it is always an emotional shock to suddenly not have a loved one with you after such a long relationship.

Sometime during the final six weeks when Jimmy was ill in bed at home, but still clear-minded and lucid, after I taught him to meditate, I had some conversations with him about death. He shared his beliefs with me, and I shared my views with him.

During one of those conversations, I mentioned to him that even though he believed as my father did — in the First Belief System — just in case he found himself still awake after he died, that my understanding was that if that's the case, then you're most likely 'an energy form' of some sort (since you wouldn't have your physical body any more), so it would seem logical that a relatively easy way to communicate with us on 'this side' would be to play around with electrical connections. Turning lights on and off. That sort of thing.

I merely mentioned it to him. Planted a seed. Sort of an experiment on my part.

After Jimmy died, his wife Donna, whom I had not told that I had had that conversation with Jimmy, told her daughter Kim (my girlfriend whom I had told about the conversation) that a couple weeks later she was on her way to meet her sister-in-law Karen for dinner one night, and while Donna was driving, the light above her head on the passenger side — you know, the ones between the driver and the passenger seats — turned on all by itself. She shook her head, and turned it off by pushing the button. Then she said, "Jimmy, is that you?" And the light on her side turned on…again, all by itself. Donna reached up and pushed the button turning it off.

It has not done that again since. So it doesn't seem to have been a short circuit in the car.

Shortly after that incident, maybe a week or so later, while Donna was in her bedroom reading in bed, the light next to the bed turned off — again, all by itself. So, she turned it back on again. There was no loose connection that she could see.

And that light has not done that again since.

Was it Jimmy playing with the electrical connections to let Donna know he was okay, that he survived his physical death? Who knows for sure.

But now that Donna knows that I planted that seed in his head, she smiles and says, "It's all your fault, Kel Chin, that Jimmy knows how to do that now!"

What's the Point?

Remember, the point of my mentioning these stories is not to convince you that they are ironclad "proof" of the continuation of the mind after the death of the body. The point is to show how these possibilities exist, and to get you to think on your own about how you might interpret these experiences yourself.

Also, if you have had similar experiences yourself, to show you that you are not alone in having them. Sometimes even that is enough to lessen the fear we may have — knowing that we are not alone in having such experiences that otherwise may be viewed by others as abnormal or weird...especially since we as a culture don't talk about them.

Another reason to share these experiences is to perhaps consider how they might impact your belief about death — especially if you are in a *hybrid* situation, where you may believe more than one of the belief systems are at play in your mind, not quite sure which way to choose. Maybe these stories will help you feel more secure in your own belief in an afterlife, for example, if you may have been leaning that way already.

And, remember, our main objective is to help us overcome the fear of death, regardless of the specific belief system we may have.

So, if you have this Third Belief System about death — where there is no fear associated with the continued existence after death, no fear of the Afterlife — the 'post-death stage' then becomes merely a transition, a comfortable transition where the mind continues its journey.

Perhaps, when the time comes, our mind will continue on its journey in a similar way as described in some of the stories we have just shared.

And, if you have ever experienced something similar to any of these experiences, I encourage you to talk about it with others. Not to convince them to believe as you do, or even that your experiences prove anything in particular, but simply to share information with others, so we aren't wound so tight worrying about death, and not talking about it. It will be good for you and for them. And I think you may find that there are more people than you realize who have had — or know of someone who has had — similar experiences.

Chapter 10

Recognition Memories

Déjà Vu?

How many of you have had this experience — where you go to a place you've never been before, and you think, "Wow. This place feels really familiar."

A lot of people have had this experience.

Sometimes we call it "Déjà Vu." But, what I'm referring to is not the 'regular' déjà vu that we experience where we think, "I feel like I've said that before." It's deeper, more tangible, more 'sticky' than that — it actually *feels* 'real.' It's almost a 'knowing' that you have been there before.

Recognition Memories

My friend Denice told me her experience about the very first time she flew into London.

She used to be a top international model. Denice is originally from Texas, but soon found herself as a young adult in her 20's living in London, England and working around the world for many years. But the first time she flew into London, she thought to herself, "I've *been here* before."

Many of us have had this type of experience.

When I was 20 years old, I went on a foreign study program in Europe. I was a French major studying in France. And since you're paying for the airfare anyway, you figure you might as well go a couple of weeks early and travel a little bit before the classes start. So we did that.

I traveled with a couple of my college buddies who were much more well-read than I ever was, and much more historically knowledgeable (they were private school kids — I was a public school kid).

We went from France and took a train down to Rome. And one of them suggested we go check out the Appian Way. I had heard of the Appian Way but didn't really know much about it, other than it had something to do with ancient Rome.

They said, "Let's go to the Appian Way and go to the catacombs." I didn't even know what the catacombs were, so I thought, "Okay," and so I'm just kind of bumming along with my two buddies.

The Catacombs

So, we got to these catacombs — the San Sebastian Catacombs. There are basically three main catacombs at mile marker one and two, just outside Rome. These catacombs were built 2,000 years ago.

For those of you who are like I was in 1971 and don't know what the catacombs are...

First of all, physically it's a labyrinth of tunnels, basically — stairways lined with small burial plots carved out of the walls, and every once in a while a few small rooms. Why small? Because all you had 2,000 years ago was a pickax, a shovel, and bucket, and you chipped away at the dirt and the rock to carve it out. There were small rooms to have meetings and ceremonies — basically what we would call today "church services."

Early Christians (and others) primarily used the catacombs to bury their dead because it was illegal to bury the dead within the city walls of Rome. Sometimes Christians would also secretly meet down there in the candlelit rooms, safe from the Roman soldiers who thought it was "too spooky" to go down there, or didn't want to get lost in the 10 miles of tunnels of darkness. In one of the three catacombs, 500,000 people are buried — that's how extensive and expansive they were.

So, back to my experience...

Keep in mind — when you're walking into the catacombs, this labyrinth of tunnels and stairways — it's pitch black. And back in 1971, there were no big crowds, no tour buses, no nothing. We just walked up — there were the three of us and maybe two or three other people on the tour. That was it, half a dozen of us with a tour guide who had a flashlight. No other equipment, no internal lighting in the catacombs.

We were walking down, way down, down — 40 feet, 50, maybe 60 feet deep (the equivalent of a 6-story building) under the earth. You walked down this long maze of tunnels, these stairways that have been rough hewn, carved out, chipped out. And 2,000-year-old bodies are buried, stacked in carved out plots in the walls with stone slabs in front of them.

As you're walking down the stairs, you can look down past these roped-off areas, and the stairs keep going into the darkness. You don't want to go down there. You'll never come back — you know you'll get lost in the many miles of tunnels.

Anyway, my point of telling you this story is that when I came back up to the surface, if you had asked me, first of all, "How long was that tour? How long were you down there, Kelvin?"

I had no idea. I was in a complete and utter 'time warp.' Ten minutes…maybe an hour and a half? I don't know, it could've been anything. [My friend later told me it was 25 minutes.]

The other thing that I remember when I came out of the catacombs is I knew that I had been there before. I just had that recognition of having been there before — a knowingness. Just like the same knowingness that I am typing this book on my laptop keyboard…how do I know that? I just do.

I *know* it.

I call that a "Recognition Memory" and I think they might be precursors to even older memories, potentially. I'm not saying that it absolutely is a glimpse of a past life memory, but it might be, because it's otherwise inexplicable.

These recognition memories are like this. You've never been someplace ever before and yet you feel this strange — because it's so very real — familiarity.

And, it might not just be a place. It could be a thing.

It could be certain jewelry, or certain types of jewelry. I have friends for whom certain things — in particular, certain rings — certain types of rings resonate with them in what they describe as a "very old and familiar way."

One friend in particular who lives near Washington, DC has for many years had a fascination with rings that are snakes, serpents — which she later found out interestingly come from ancient Egypt but were commonly sold in First Century ancient Rome. Her name is Josephine, and her story appears later in this book.

Again, these are just more data points, as I say. More for us to think about and discuss.

The Museum of Fine Arts

When I was little, about 6 or 7 years old, my mom — remember, she was a true Renaissance woman — would take me to the Museum of Fine Arts in Boston — the "MFA." This was back in the days before it became 'in vogue' to go to museums. Back then in the 1950's, it was like, "Who goes to museums? You look at old stuff there — big deal — paintings and old dusty stuff."

It wasn't as cool to do as it is now.

We would get there before the museum even opened, and we'd go there often because it was so easy...

My grandmother, my father's mother ("Gnin" we called her in Toisanese, a village dialect of Cantonese) lived in a red brick apartment six or eight blocks directly across the street from the museum. She would babysit my younger sister, while my dad would go off and do his 'guy thing' — you know, probably looking for new hubcaps for his car, a new chamois or something like that (he literally hand-washed his car every day regardless of weather, even in the winter!) — and then my mom and I would go to the MFA. It was the proverbial win-win for everyone involved.

I still remember it like it was yesterday.

This was our routine every time — my mom and I would go into the museum lobby and pause....

I had a Mickey Mouse watch — Mickey had bright red shorts, and white gloves. And my mom would say, "When Mickey's little hand is on the 11 and his big hand is on the 12, Kelvin, I'll meet you back here." And she would go off to look at her favorite section of paintings in the museum.

Don't forget — I was 6 or 7 years old. If you did that today, your kid would probably end up in Child Protective Services…!! Nobody would do that today, but it was different then.

And here's the interesting thing…I would routinely go to two areas.

I would go hang out with the Egyptian mummies and the Medieval armor. That's what I would do every visit — and I would hang out there for hours.

Back then, like I said, museums were not that popular, so there weren't even a lot of security guards around. So basically, I'm a 6-year-old kid hanging out all by himself in a huge museum. I would see an adult, typically a security guard, maybe once during that couple hours. They'd stroll through and they'd see me. They kind of recognized me… "Oh, him again…."

What is noteworthy (and strangely odd in how natural it felt) was that I would feel completely 'at home' in those two areas of the museum — ancient Egypt and the Medieval armor. That was the odd memory that I have about that experience. I remember feeling really, really at home with 3,500-year-old bags of dust — which, on its surface, I admit is kind of strange. It felt as if I was hanging out with long lost family members. And the Medieval armor felt completely familiar to me, even at that very young age — long before I became interested in studying about knights, or reading books about them a couple years later.

The Moons of Jupiter

Here is another experience that could fall into this "Recognition Memory" category —

I have a really good friend. His nephew, whom I've met a number of times, is now three and a half years old. I've known this little boy since he was two, so I've known him for about a year and a half now. For some inexplicable reason, this little boy is really into astronomy to the point where he knows everything about the moons of Jupiter and corrects adults about scientific issues related to the moons of Jupiter.

I didn't even know how many moons were there, but I knew Jupiter had some moons. But this kid has got it all down.

Has he ever seen the Discovery Channel? Yeah, he's probably seen the Discovery Channel once or twice. Did they drill into him the moons of Jupiter when he was two years old? Probably not.

And even if they tried to, how many two-year-olds are walking around with this plethora of knowledge about the moons of Jupiter?

It's unusual. To say the least.

Walking in a Dust Storm

My daughter Samantha has had this memory her entire life. And since she always thought it was from her childhood when she was in Las Vegas, Nevada, she never thought to mention it to her mother or myself until two years ago when she was 19 years old.

Sam says she has had this memory for as long as she has remembered anything — maybe from as young as 2 or 3 years old. She remembers walking in a dust storm next to a cart, holding the hand of an adult who is walking next to her, and holding a doll in her other hand. They are walking with a group of people across a large sandy spacious spread of land — no paved roads, no vehicles. Her recollection is that sand is blowing in their faces, and her hair is blowing in the wind. She doesn't see the face of the adult holding her hand, but she says, "My whole life I've assumed that it was either mom or you walking next to me, or [your friend] George."

Sam describes the cart as having two wheels, and says, "It's like those carts that are in shopping malls, in the large hallways that vendors sell stuff from." But the wooden cart in her memory is old and weathered.

Since she was born in Las Vegas, she has always assumed we took her out for a walk there on a day when it was windy and dust or sand was blowing in her face.

Sounds logical, right? I mean, Las Vegas is in the desert and it does get windy there. Seems like a good explanation?

Well, not exactly.

You see, we moved the family from Las Vegas to Los Angeles when Sam was about six or seven months old — she wasn't even walking yet! Plus, when she told her mom and me this memory, our first reaction was, "No way would we as parents have taken a 2-3 year old child out in a sandstorm ANYWHERE — that would NOT be good parenting!"

And, there were no sandstorms in Los Angeles — we lived in Mar Vista. Finally, we never have taken her out walking next to a cart.

So, it definitely wasn't us.

Where was Sam's memory from?

She doesn't know for sure yet. But she is pretty confident now that it is an old memory. From a different time. Not from anything she has ever read or been read to about. Because for her, the memory is so vivid, so real.

And so for now, Sam is enjoying the memory, seeing where it may take her, seeing how it may develop further. Seeing if it may eventually tell her more about herself — if it may inform her more about her personality, more about who she is now as Samantha Chin.

Again, these are just more data points. It makes you wonder. It makes you ask, "What's up with that? How do you explain these things?"

"Proof of Heaven"

In 2008, a neurosurgeon "died" physically, and went into a coma for seven days with a rare form of a brain illness. When he came back from his NDE, he wrote a book called *"Proof of Heaven."* His name is Eben Alexander, MD.

What I find interesting about his description of this life-changing experience is that he initially started out like my father, a staunch believer in what I refer to as the First Belief System about death. Dr. Alexander considered himself a neuroscientist first and foremost, notwithstanding his strong Christian beliefs and practice.

Yet, after his NDE which he vividly describes in his book, his belief about death and dying changed dramatically. Now, based on his experiences during that coma, Dr. Alexander believes that there is an Afterlife. And, most importantly, he has no fear of death.

The other main point I like to share with my audiences is that Dr. Alexander's very personal, detailed description of what he calls "Heaven," is exactly that — it is his *personal* experience of it.

It is not necessarily how it is for everyone.

I think his experience is genuine. It is what he experienced. And he interprets that experience in the way he describes to us. But that does not necessarily mean that everyone will experience what he calls the post-physical death transition stage and "heaven" in the same way that he did.

Let me explain further what I mean…

Structure of the Afterlife

I think there is a general structure to the Afterlife experience that everyone shares — a feeling of expansiveness of the mind, peacefulness and freedom — all of which I think comes from not having a physical body any more. However, *how* each of us experiences that is unique to each of us. There is not *one* way. There are *many* ways that can be experienced.

Think about it in the following way —

In much the same way, we all share a common description of being awake — there is a certain focus to our waking state. If we hit our hand on a table, it won't merely pass through it. And if we drive through an intersection, we should pay attention so we don't hit another car. Those are similar structural characteristics to being awake — the need to focus, solid objects are hard, and paying attention to traffic is important.

But, the actual *experience* of being awake is as varied as the number of people there are on the planet.

For example, two people may drive through the same intersection at the same time but have a totally different experience of doing so. I may be focused on the green light changing to yellow, and my passenger may be focused on seeing the street sign or the clothes in a store window.

Which of those two experiences of driving through that intersection is the "correct" experience? I would say that both are correct, or at least as valid as the other.

And both sets of experiences have a shared common structure to them. That structure is what we can all agree on.

In that same way, there is no *correct* experience of the Afterlife that *is the way it is.*

Too much attention tends to be placed on the "What." People tend to get hung up in arguing about the correct description of exactly what the experience will be like when we die.

I think that attention is misplaced.

What is important is to make sure that we have done our internal work *before* we die, so that when we die — i.e., when our physical bodies die — we will have no fear of the Afterlife because having established an inner security and self-confidence by 'turning within' regularly, we will be able to handle *whatever* unknowns present themselves to us.

So, even though we may espouse the Third Belief System — that after death, the mind continues, and perhaps, it transitions — into what, we may not be sure — we will do so with that unwavering confidence that we will have developed throughout our life on the planet — before we die.

Chapter 11

The Fourth Belief System

"My mind continues after my body dies.
I transition to a place.
Maybe I vacation for a while — chill out, rest,
rejuvenate — and then I choose to 'reincarnate'
and come back in another physical body and live
another lifetime."

Past Lives or Reincarnation

Some of you may have heard the term "past lives," or "future lives." That is another way of describing the belief of those who hold this Fourth Belief System. They believe in the idea of reincarnation.

So, their belief is that after they physically die, their mind (or soul if you prefer that terminology) continues on to some place that they may label or define in a number of ways, depending on their particular religious or spiritual background. Their mind stays there for a while, sometimes a short time, sometimes for many years. And, at some point for whatever reason — perhaps they may want to connect with some old friends again — they decide to come back in another body and live another lifetime in physical form.

University of Virginia Medical School

Since 1967, the University of Virginia Medical School has had a unit to document and research the purported past life memories of children, especially between the ages of 2-5. It is located in the medical school's Psychiatric and Neurobehavioral Sciences Department, Division of Perceptual Studies and was originally founded as a research unit by Ian Stevenson, MD, a Canadian-born U.S. psychiatrist.

The Division's research staff has been investigating these cases since 1961, and have published numerous books and articles about them.

Dr. Stevenson, who passed away in 2007 at age 88, became known internationally for his research into reincarnation, and the idea that emotions, memories, and even physical injuries can be transferred from one life to another. He traveled extensively over a period of forty years, investigating 3,000 cases of children around the world who claimed to remember past lives. In some cases, he would travel to the city in the world with the child, and often the child would point out specific places where things happened and frequently the child would bring up dates, cite names and details. He was a very careful investigator. He wrote in an academic style, similar to a lawyer, providing evidence of each case, including witnesses and having the child take a lie detector test. He maintained his objectivity throughout.

For example, one 2-year-old child in Louisiana named James Leininger first started having nightmares of being in an airplane on fire — "Airplane crash! Plane on fire! Little man can't get out!" This nightmare recurred 4-5 nights a week. When his mother asked him who the 'little man' was, James said, "Me." When his dad asked who shot his plane down, he said, "the Japanese." And when his dad asked how he knew it was the Japanese, he said, "the big red sun."

He was recalling being a fighter pilot in World War II, and "the big red sun" referred to the insignia on all Japanese warplanes. He also remembered the names of his fallen pilot friends who died before he did — naming his three GI Joe dolls "Billy, Leon and Walter." When his parents asked why he named them those unusual names, he said, "...because that is who met me when I got to heaven." His dad later confirmed that these three fighter pilots from James' ship were named Billy Peeler, Leon Connor and Walter Devlin. Little James even matched the dolls with their hair color accurately: dark hair (Billy), blonde (Leon), and reddish (Walter). He also was taken to see a vintage fighter at a war museum, similar to that which he claimed to have once flown, and as he simulated doing a pre-flight check of the plane, he pointed out various mechanical issues of the plane in detail (e.g., tires blowing out on landing, and veering to the left, both of which that plane had an initial tendency to do, his dad later found out).

Remember, the child was only 2 years old.

He recalled other very specific details — being shot down by the Japanese near Iwo Jima (he recognized it in a photograph), that he flew off a "boat called the Natoma" (which was later corroborated as an aircraft carrier called the "USS Natoma Bay" that was involved in the Battle of Iwo Jima), that his name was James and that he was "the third James."

His father looked this information up and discovered there was only one pilot from the USS Natoma Bay who had been shot down and killed in that battle over Iwo Jima on March 3, 1945, and his name was "James Huston, Jr." So, that would make this young Louisiana boy the third James after James Huston's father, James Huston, Sr.

He also said his friend was named "Jack Larsen." And when Huston was shot down, the pilot of the plane flying next to his was Jack Larsen.

According to another eyewitness Ralph Clarver, a rear gunner in a TBM Avenger torpedo bomber also flying right next to the plane flown by James Huston, Clarver's description of Huston's plane getting hit matched James Leininger's description almost exactly: "Hit in the engine, exploding into fire, crashing into the water and quickly sinking."

Do these facts sound incredible? Imagine if this was your child telling you these stories. How would you handle it? Especially if reincarnation did not fit within your belief system.

In fact, the young boy's father happened to be a devout Christian whose religious beliefs conflicted with reincarnation, causing him great personal struggle. Yet, his son's detailed memories and emotional connections with events that happened fifty years earlier could not be otherwise explained. So, the father and mother were so moved by it, that they felt they had to believe their child — saying that, "He could not have learned this from watching Sesame Street!"

They then tracked down James Huston's now elderly surviving sister, Anne, and brought their son James to meet with her. He proceeded to tell his parents her name wasn't "Anne"...it was "Annie." Anne later told them that only her brother James called her by the name, "Annie." He also told them, "She wasn't my oldest sister. I had an older sister than that, her name was Ruth," which Anne confirmed. Then, he told Anne facts about his life growing up as a young boy as James Huston (detailed facts which Anne corroborated), and about their family that only she and her siblings knew — for example, asking her, "Where's the picture that mom painted of you?" No one else knew of the existence of that painting, besides Anne, James, Ruth, and their mother.

On a related note, James said that he picked his current parents before he was born when he saw them in what he referred to as "in the big pink hotel." It turns out that his parents were vacationing at the Royal Hawaiian Hotel in Hawaii on Waikiki five weeks before his mother became pregnant with him. His parents never told him about that vacation or hotel. The Royal Hawaiian Hotel is famous for its oceanfront splendor, its tradition as a Hawaiian institution since 1927, and especially its bright pink color, the color of flamingoes. It is known as "the Pink Palace of the Pacific."

The University of Virginia Medical School has collected hundreds of similar accounts. You can read more on their website and draw your own conclusions.

Josephine and Lucius

A friend of mine in Maryland had this experience when napping about two years ago. In her dream, she was sleeping and was woken up by flooding in her house.

She described it to me as follows —

"I was having a bad dream of dying in a flooded room. I forced myself to wake up [in the dream], or so I thought I was [awake]. I got out of bed, walked into the other room, which was like a big open temple of another era, and I seemed to be in sort of its basement guiding people to a stairway to safety, but I was drowning because the water kept rising. And then, I saw a man standing in a white tunic. I distinctly remember thinking how absolutely handsome he was. He had blonde curly hair and a bearded face. I was fascinated by *how blonde his hair was*. I even reached out to touch his hair because it looked so glorious. He also had a plaque on his neck and I vaguely remember reading "wisdom, wealth…" — it was bronze and intricate. This image basically made me think he was a god or angel, and he said to me, 'How do you expect to see your Past Life if you're too scared to see past your death in a nightmare?'"

At that point, she realized she was not in fact awake, but was still dreaming, and just was *awake in her dream.*

When Josephine actually woke up, she didn't think much of it — until she searched online typing in the search window the words "bearded, blonde, curly"… and a photo of a marble portrait from a bust or statue of *the same man* she saw in her dream popped up on her computer screen.

She didn't know who he was until she added the word "Roman" to her search. And the name "Lucius Verus" appeared.

Following a simple suggestion I had given her a couple of weeks earlier, to "Follow the bread crumbs" if something unusual happens, she looked up who Lucius Verus was. It turns out he was co-emperor for a short while with (and was the stepbrother of) the Roman Emperor Marcus Aurelius.

And most interestingly, Lucius had a fascination with his own blondness — to such a great extent that he was known to have added gold dust to his hair and beard to make it appear even more yellow and blonde than it already naturally did. He was also known for his incredible good looks, which he regularly used to his advantage with women.

Lucius also had a mistress named Panthea, who famously made Lucius — the historians tell us — "shave off his long barbarian-like beard."

Interestingly, before Josephine laid down to nap, she had said to herself, "I wonder what my past life was like…." So, in a sense, she may have planted a seed to encourage the surfacing of a memory.

She also mentioned that she had what she described as "a millisecond déjà vu" that matched that beard-shaving event on the same day she spoke with me — two weeks earlier, before she ever knew of Lucius Verus or of this beard-shaving by Panthea.

Is that dream and are those experiences proof that Josephine was Panthea, and had a prior relationship with Lucius Verus in a past life?

No, not necessarily.

But again, it is an interesting data point and an unusual body of synchronous and coincidental experiences. And I think it very well could represent how we begin to recover these old memories — i.e., a little at a time, through random occurrences that trigger them, and often in a nonlinear fashion…much like we remember any memories, including those from this lifetime.

Yahoo News

On Yahoo News early in 2015, there was a story about a young boy. The story originally aired on FOX-TV. The boy, Luke Ruehlman, is now around 5 years old, but when his experiences started happening he was about 2 years old.

What happened was this little boy in suburban Cincinnati, Ohio started telling his mother what she first considered imaginary stories. He would sit on her lap, and she'd be putting on her makeup, and he would say, "Oh, I used to have earrings like those. I like those earrings. Those look just like my old earrings."

Of course, she just thought he's got a good imagination, "he's telling stories to mom." However, the story details started developing and month after month, he began telling his mom more and more.

For example, "When I was a girl, I used to have black hair," etc.

And then there were these odd fixations. First it was on safety, being very careful with everyone he was with when crossing the street, then with anything hot, or with anything to do with tall things, heights — and then on the name Pam. He named his stuffed ladybug Pam, and soon everything was "Pam" this and that.

When his mom, Erika, asked him who Pam was, he said, "Well I used to be, I died, but I went up to heaven, I saw God, and he pushed me back down and when I woke up, I was a baby and you named me Luke."

So, over a number of months, he started giving her these bits of information — more and more data points.

His mom started thinking there may be something to this. Getting more curious, she asked him if he remembered how he died. And Luke said, "Yes, in a fire..." (then he made a motion with his hand like he was jumping off a tall building). Later he said, "It was a tall building in a big city..." and that he remembered walking a lot and taking a train. Then, in another of these many brief conversations, he told her, "It was in Chicago."

Eventually, while she was still skeptical, she had enough data points to go research this herself.

And she soon discovered there was a woman named Pamela Robinson who died jumping out of a 4th floor window of a burning Chicago hotel in 1993 — the Hotel Paxton, which was located in a predominantly African-American neighborhood. It was the worst fire in the city's recent memory, and nineteen people died.

That's when Erika asked her son, "Luke, what color was Pam's skin?" And he looked right up at her and said, "Duh, black."

That's when Erika's mother suggested that she contact Pam Robinson's surviving family. When she did, she found out even more similarities — that Pam was a keyboard player and was a big Stevie Wonder fan.

Coincidentally, the young Luke was known to carry around a toy keyboard everywhere he went, and loved Stevie Wonder music. Not a typical music genre or artist for a 2-year-old Caucasian boy in suburban Cincinnati to be fond of in 2012.

Furthermore, on the Lifetime Channel, Luke was featured on a TV show where he was given a sheet of a dozen photographs, and asked to point out anyone he recognized. While on camera, he is heard saying, "I know someone I can recognize. I remember when this was taken…" And, he correctly pointed to the picture of Pam Robinson.

Luke's Fixation

Note that Luke also had a fixation, maybe a fear of heights and hot things, certainly a strong concern about them. And, according to his mother, this was totally random, completely 'out of the blue.' He had not had any bad or fearful experiences related to heights or fire in his life so far. Yet he had those fixations.

Could they have been from his past life experience? It seems likely.

I point this out because some of you may have similar odd, completely random fears about death or dying that, at least according to your life so far, have no bearing or connection with any experience you know of that you have had. Yet, your fear is very real, and may even be specific to a source (a place, type of event, genre of music, etc.) or type of fear (flying, swimming, water, falling, etc.).

In fact, I have spoken and worked with many people from around the world who have contacted me through our Foundation website who have expressed such fears, often of death and dying. Their parents and friends are all completely healthy. Their grandparents may even still be alive. And they have never had any traumatic experiences themselves that they are aware of. Yet, they have this sometimes paralyzing fear of death.

These inexplicable fears may sometimes be associated with a memory either from this lifetime that we have forgotten or suppressed, or from another lifetime that we have similarly forgotten or suppressed. By simply entertaining this possibility, we can sometimes begin to loosen the grip of that fear on us. And sometimes, by 'turning within' through various modalities, meditation and other means, we may be able to unlock those old memories and release ourselves from the binding effect of those ancient experiences.

Proof of Other Lifetimes?

Again, is all of this proof of other lifetimes?

Not necessarily, but it certainly raises questions.

You may not have heard of these types of experiences before. But, since a large segment of the world population (12-44%, depending on which country...it's 20% in the United States) believes in reincarnation, it's valuable to have at least a basic understanding of this Fourth Main Belief System about death.

So, at the very least, a discussion of this Fourth Belief System raises the issue of Past Lives, and brings the concept into the forefront of our awareness. And it certainly makes us wonder.

Could we have been here before in another lifetime? Might we come back again in a different body in 20, 50, 150, 500 years from now?

Could a better understanding of our past lives help us overcome inexplicable fears? Logically, it does not make sense that we would have a fear of death itself if we believed this Fourth Belief System (because in this belief, the person/mind does not die). However, we may have fears that are related to dying, as in Luke's fixation, that are alleviated or eliminated by recognizing and releasing oneself from the source of that fear.

Chapter 12

What's the Value of
Past Lives?

What's the Value of Past Lives?

Let's assume that past lives exist. Just for the sake of our discussion, and for those who do hold this Fourth Belief System, let's look at the "So what?" question.

What I like to focus on is the practical. I am a pragmatist — what's the practical value of having memories about past lives?

Because what did I say at the very beginning of our discussion? I said that it's about now. It's about *living in the continual present*. That's where we're living our lives.

We're not living our life in the past. We're living our life in the present, but what can we learn from the past? What more can we each learn about ourselves — from our memories perhaps — from our past — whether it's from our past in this lifetime or another lifetime?

We can always learn more about our personalities that can help each of us live a more productive, effective, happier life in the continual present, in the now. That's the value of knowing one's self better, and in applying that now.

A Carthage Memory

I have a memory from a long time ago that I started recalling when I was in my 20's.

I remembered being a slave on a Carthaginian warship.

The interesting thing was that I didn't know where Carthage was when I first started having this memory. I didn't know any history about it. I hadn't read a lot of ancient history. But somehow I had this memory — it just came out of nowhere.

People have sometimes asked me, "When and how does this happen? How do memories of what seem to be 'past lives' come about?"

My experience was that, when it first started happening in my 20's, it often happened during meditation, or sometimes afterwards during the rest period lying down that I always take after I meditate. Later, as I began to become more comfortable with it, memories would sometimes appear when I was sleeping and dreaming, or at other similar times when I was just in a quiet moment. Then, these experiences of past memories would begin to surface even in my activity — in the shower, or when I was just walking around in a relatively unfocused, open-minded state.

Now it can happen to me pretty much anytime, even if I'm not in a quiet moment. But at first it would happen more often when I was quiet inside.

And it comes in many forms. Sometimes it's a visual image, other times it's a feeling of familiarity with something, and still other times it comes in the form of a 'knowingness' about a certain factoid — e.g., a role I had, a period in history in which I lived, certain people I was with, or specific food I ate (sometimes food that I have never eaten this lifetime).

As I became more familiar and at ease with these recollections, they would come more frequently with greater detail and coloration, and often with the full range of emotions and physical senses — touch, taste, smell, hearing, seeing.

As I said, this Carthaginian memory started happening when I was in my 20's some time in the mid-1970's. I remembered that I was a slave on a Carthaginian warship. I was black, I was African, and I was enslaved, chained down as a rower on the ship. I was fed pretty well, not fancy, but they kept us fed and we were in really good physical shape — for as long as we lived anyway.

We were often in battle on the Mediterranean in the Carthaginian wars — or as they are historically known — the Punic Wars. I found out what the wars were called many years later when I researched this.

These three wars between Rome and Carthage took place about 2200 years ago, between 264 BC and

146 BC. They were likely the largest wars ever to have taken place at that time in world history. It was not uncommon for 10,000 to 30,000 men to die in one day of battle, with the Romans losing somewhere between 50,000 to 80,000 men in one land battle at the Battle of Cannae in southeastern Italy, where they were outmaneuvered by the significantly outnumbered Carthaginian general, Hannibal, in what was one of the earliest known uses of the battle tactics called "pincer movements."

During that lifetime, however, I was a slave in the Carthaginian navy, which dominated battle on the Mediterranean and kept all the shipping lanes free for their commerce.

What I remembered was that the primary mode of navy battle was to row as fast as you could, and then you slammed into the other ship. You rammed the other ship with this major wooden ramming device on the bow of your ship encased in metal — that was the technique — and you punctured the other ship to sink it or to board it.

Sometimes you would throw hot oil on the other ship and then shoot an arrow or throw a torch over and then the other ship would blow up. It would be on fire — aflame. That happened to my ship.

Sometimes you lose in battle. Sometimes you get hurt. Sometimes you die.

What I remembered was surviving.

I was either one of the few survivors, or the sole survivor on my ship. I just remember being alone on a piece of wreckage, about a 4 foot by 6 foot piece of the ship, clinging to it in the Mediterranean. And I remember how hot it was. I remember the physical sensation of getting basically roasted in the sun, totally exposed — the physical pain and mental anguish. Primarily I remember the mental anguish.

But, I survived.

The Practical Value of Past Life Memories

What is most significant from this Carthage memory that is *valuable for me today* is that I remember my willpower to survive, my mental 'will to live.' I recall how I realized then that what was critical was 'between my ears.' That it was not a physical thing, that it was a mental thing controlling my physical.

The other thing I remember is that somehow I used my wits — my mind — to survive that horrific life and death experience and to make it to shore or to get close enough to some other ships to be rescued. Whereas, I could have psychologically — mentally — given up at any time and drowned. But I didn't.

That has served me *this* lifetime when I have been laid off from work five times, from companies and law firms going through economic challenges — e.g., the 2000 dot-com bubble bursting, the 2008 global financial crisis, company mergers, etc. I have survived that and supported a family of four, notwithstanding having been hit with these potentially catastrophic experiences — experiences that were not only financially devastating, but were also emotionally challenging.

That experience from my past has strengthened me by showing me what I have been capable of withstanding in the past, and therefore informing me more deeply about who I am today. It showed me how the power of my mind — in what many would call a "no-win" situation — kept me alive, even though my physical body was badly injured in one of life's most dire situations — adrift alone and unknown on a vast sea during a huge wartime battle.

That's my point of giving that example. Because to me, it's about the pragmatism of that recollection, the practical application of that past memory *in my current here and now.*

What do we learn about ourselves from similar memories? About how we 'tick'? And from perhaps how we have survived in the past or handled a difficult situation in the past?

It might not be a survival issue. It might be, for example, some intense emotional issue that you dealt with and handled in the past. And in your current life, perhaps it informs you and helps you deal in a more healthy way with a similar emotionally traumatic experience you may be dealing with today.

Or, how understanding a past relationship might inform a current one and help us in moving forward with it. Perhaps even a relationship that you may remember was with that same person in another lifetime where relevant personality traits played a key part in how the relationship played out and is now again presently playing out.

But the point is that it's that *practical* application that I suggest we look for.

How can it help us *today?*

Otherwise, as I often say, "It's just cocktail party talk. Who cares?"

And, as I have emphasized, it is not about living in the past.

It is about applying those memories that may come from past lives to our current life — helping us better navigate our lives in the continual present. Again, that is the key because that will also increase the likelihood that such memories will help us live happier, more productive and enjoyable lives — in my case, as Kelvin Chin.

And, one important *caveat* on Past Lives, and a reminder regarding any and all of these experiences and perspectives —

As you know, this book and all that I teach is nonreligious and non-belief based. Some of my own personal experiences seem to fit into this conceptual framework of past lives. And so I have interpreted them in that way.

If you do not believe in past lives, I am not suggesting that you have to. Even I am not *bound* by the belief in anything — including past lives. For me, increasing our understanding is a fluid process, not static. Right now, the concept of past lives fits with my experiences that I recall, which are otherwise unexplainable.

That said, I encourage all of us to continue to explore ourselves and understand ourselves better — *in whatever way fits best for each of us.*

Chapter 13

Other Values of Past Life Memories

The Eternal Mind

Scientists and theologians alike speak about a "start" to the Universe, the "Big Bang Theory" as the most popular commonly discussed idea. This is an intriguing idea.

But is it accurate? Does it make sense? Does it fit with the "First Law of Thermodynamics" in physics — that neither energy nor matter can really be created or destroyed?

First of all, the Big Bang Theory focuses on physical reality. What about the mind?

The First Law of Thermodynamics tells us that even if we can't "see" the physical object that may have been destroyed, its energy still exists somewhere.

So, where does that lead us? Let's examine whether or not life itself is possibly eternal — whether the physical and mental energy that exists in the Universe may actually be a constant that has always existed and never will be destroyed.

Is life eternal?

Many people believe that life is eternal. They may come to that conclusion through different routes.

For example, some may believe that other lives go on and on after one dies, i.e., life on the planet still continues after death — those people may each view themselves individually as non-eternal, but that life in the form of *other* people's lives will continue after they die. To them, this is a form of eternal life, where there is still conservation of the energy that was their life, in the form of others who may come after them.

Yet other people may believe that their own lives may continue on after death — the idea of an afterlife like heaven, or perhaps even reincarnation. In that latter belief system, as in this Fourth Belief System, there is a belief that the energy continues and the 'personality' may also continue afterwards in yet a different physical form, a different body and a different lifetime.

The First Law of Thermodynamics states that —

Energy can be changed from one form to another, but it cannot be created or destroyed. The total amount of energy and matter in the Universe remains constant, merely changing from one form to another.

Essentially, it says that we are energy. Yes, we have bodies, but even our bodies are made up of energy — molecules, atoms, other small particles.

So, if our energy cannot be created or destroyed, perhaps we simply change form. We may debate, depending on what our belief system is, "what form" we change into. But, the First Law of Thermodynamics seems to indicate that energy is not lost — because no energy in the universe is gained or lost. It is the same energy that has always existed.

In any of those cases then, where the belief is that life is eternal, there can be no beginning or end. Because that is the very definition of the word "eternal."

So, another value of remembering our past lives is that it seems to be consistent with this notion of eternal life — this idea that maybe our minds do continue after we die, maybe they are eternal, maybe they continue on forever, and that maybe our personalities pretty much stay the same for a very long, long time.

This is what I think, happens — this has been what I have observed in myself through my memories — that my personality generally stays the same.

Yes, it incrementally may change over time somewhat, not absolutely staying the same, but pretty much the same. And we can choose to express it in different ways in different lifetimes through different bodies — male, female, change gender, change roles, type of role in society, etc. — over these long, long periods of time.

Experimenting With Our Minds to Enjoy Life

What is another reason why it may be valuable to remember our past lives?

Because I think our existence is about enjoying life and experimenting.

After all, what is more fun than using yourself in your own experiment? Experimenting with yourself in as many ways that you can imagine.

If that's the case, then of course there should be no fear of death, because death is merely a transition — it's just a stopping point or pausing point between lives — if you believe in the Fourth Belief System.

Building Our Self-Confidence

As I have discussed earlier using my Carthaginian slave memory as an example, a third value of remembering our past lives is that practical benefit of accruing more *knowledge about ourselves*.

So that in *Knowing Thyself*, we may grow in our inner strength and self-confidence. We may, for example, gain this from memories of successes, or from overcoming significant life challenges in the past. Or alternatively, from recalling the source experience of something we had up to that point perceived as a weakness in ourselves today, thereby perhaps freeing ourselves from the grip of that experience by gaining greater clarity about ourselves now through that memory, and how that need not define who we are in the present.

The bottom line —

In deriving that from our memories, we can then each carry forward that greater self-knowledge, and apply it in our lives *today.*

Being Creative, Having Fun

Another benefit I would say is just the fun of it — the enjoyability factor — the ability to be creative.

When you have more memories of what, how and who you may have been, it opens us up inside. It can make us feel less restricted, less constricted — especially when we realize through our own recollections that we have been much more than what we have perceived in this lifetime alone.

And, is it important to be absolutely sure that all the details of our memories are fully accurate? I don't think so. Much in the same way that the details of our recollections about *this current* lifetime are not always fully accurate or that important.

Because again, what have we said is most important? *Living in the present — in the here and the now.*

So really being sure about the minute details of what might be a memory or might be a past life is much less important than if your experiences — your memories — *inform you further about who you are* and if they *help you be happier now.*

So, another benefit of recalling our past life memories is to be more conscious about our creativity — i.e., the creativity of our own lifetimes as we go through them.

What I'm suggesting is that perhaps instead of stumbling through our lives haphazardly and unconsciously, we may instead take hold of "all of that which we are" — meaning all of those memories and self-knowledge that comes along with it — and go through our future lives in a more conscious way. Sort of look at each of ourselves as being creative artists, being in the creative arts — but being the creative artist *of ourselves, or creating ourselves.* Because I think that may actually reflect the truth more than we may have realized.

Each of us is our own Leonardo da Vinci — we need to just grab hold of that awareness, and enjoy life through that new lens. Through that new way of looking at ourselves, our Free Will to create, and our gathering of self-knowledge (the paint for the canvas), and then 'painting our lives' each moment of this lifetime (and other lifetimes going forward) with that new flair for living.

We can create ourselves in whatever form we really want to. The more clarity we may have with our memories, the more fun, I think, we can have with that creative process.

It's like thinking, "Wow, let's figure out how many more ways I can be creative with expressing myself!"

Sometimes people metaphorically talk about expressing themselves as, say, "an actor." I think all of us may eventually discover that we are expressing ourselves as 'actors through eternity' — through our different lifetimes.

Transition or Vacation?

Maybe our physical death is just sort of a 'milestone' for that particular lifetime — and then we go into a transition stage. We go 'on vacation' between lives.

This is what I think happens. This is what I have some recollections of. We go on vacation.

Some in our culture may want to call it "Heaven." You can call it whatever. Any label works. The folks who are 'minding the store on the other side' don't care what we call it, and they will use whatever term we like to make us feel comfortable, because I think it's just a comfort zone to hang out in, so to speak. And then we can choose to stay there or not. We can come back into physical form in another lifetime if we want.

No Fear of Death

So, that's the Fourth Belief System — reincarnation, past lives, future lives, or staying on vacation on 'the other side.'

And there should be no fear of death, because if you have this belief system, you do not die. Your mind lives eternally — whether it chooses to take a physical form or whether it chooses to stay on the nonphysical side of the curtain.

Chapter 14

Final Thoughts

Overcoming the Fear of Death Through Any of the 4 Main Belief Systems

Again, what's the point? The point is not that you have to believe in past lives, or even believe in some form of an afterlife. You can believe just like my father did — that this is it — that the brain and mind are inextricably connected.

That's totally fine. But the message is still the same — figure out what your belief system is, and apply the suggested insights and understandings that we discussed in this book to reduce and overcome your fear of death.

Free Will — It is Your Decision, Your Choice

Stay within your own belief system if that is where your comfort zone is. Do not go outside your belief system simply because your friends or family try to convince you to.

Own whatever decision you make.

Yes, you can change it at any time, of course. But this is all about figuring out what works for each of us — and we *each* have to figure that out *for ourselves.* Because how much more personal can you get than dealing with your own beliefs about your own death?

Live Life Now

And remember, another big message is to live life, *live life now.* The pursuit of happiness is all about *living in the present.*

This is what it's about. So reduce and overcome the fear of death by getting more clarity on what your belief system is. And increase your understanding about how to overcome your fear through the lens of *your particular belief system.*

Turn Within

Finally, be sure to 'turn within' — through whatever effortless way works best for you — to experientially increase your inner strength and confidence, and eliminate the stress and anxiety from your mind, body and emotions to help create and sustain more balance in your life.

These are the keys to *permanently* overcoming our fear of death. To reclaiming the power of life over death.

Epilogue

The Implications

If we each start to think more clearly through our own belief lens about our fear of death, and as we open ourselves to understanding more about other people's beliefs about death, we will naturally develop more compassion for others. The perceived threat to our survival that triggers the "fight or flight" response in us will subside. Our own fears about death will no longer get in our way to feel and think more clearly, not only about ourselves but also about others.

We will naturally become more emotionally present, and pragmatically helpful to ourselves, as well as our friends and loved ones.

We will become better caregivers in the process. Whether we are professional caregivers or not, we all will become 'caregivers' at some point in our lives for someone — our grandparents, parents, children, friends, and perhaps even a stranger who has no one else for support.

So it is incumbent on all of us as a society to consider, ponder and digest the full range of thoughts being discussed on death and dying, and to build upon these thoughts with each of our own thoughts. And to think about how we each can contribute to improving our world by reducing and eliminating the fear of death — first within ourselves, then in those we touch throughout our lives.

For in doing so, we will all then participate in creating a world society that embraces life more fully, and includes death and dying as a natural part of that process of living. Not as something separate and isolated from life itself.

In this way, we can use our joint effort in overcoming the fear of death to help all of us come together — across our various religions, cultures, and beliefs — building relationships and institutions throughout the world that reflect this more respectful and inclusionary perspective on death and dying.

Appendix I

Note on "Related Fears" to the Fear of Death

For the keys to overcoming the fears that are *related to* the fear of death (but are not the actual "fear of death") — e.g., the fear of pain and suffering, the fear of losing a loved one, the fear of inadequacy in helping a loved one at their time of death, the fear of punishment, and the fear of eternity — I welcome you to explore my second book that will cover these important "related fears" to the fear of death: *Reclaiming the Power of Life Over Death By Overcoming Fears Related to Dying.*

Appendix II

Discussion Groups

As I mentioned early in this book, I think our culture would benefit tremendously from more discussion about death and dying. Instead of sticking our 'head in the sand,' thinking that it will go away, we should talk about it.

Because it won't go away. That is the one thing we can all guarantee!

So, to that end, I encourage you to create your own local "Overcoming the Fear of Death" discussion groups to continue the discussion we have started together in this book. Alternatively, add the ideas I have introduced here to your own discussions you may already be having at your neighborhood hospice, cancer support or other groups.

Feel free to use my book as a catalyst or as a focal center to begin having your discussions around. Disagree with what I say, or come up with your own versions and interpretations of what I describe in the book.

Take any approach you think that helps the discourse.

I don't mind at all!

My role is to start us thinking more cogently and more thoughtfully about death and dying. And if my book has contributed to that end, to whatever degree, then my objective has been met, our Foundation's mission has been furthered.

So, please take it upon yourselves to continue this discussion. Take a leadership role in your respective communities — wherever you are in the world — and help others, and yourselves, explore their thinking about death and dying.

And remember, be open to hearing what other people have to say. We are all in this together trying to figure out how best to improve our *views* on death and dying, as well as our *practices* related to this important time of life.

I hope this book has helped you further that goal.

We will all benefit from your continued work — both as you work on yourself internally and with others externally.

Appendix III

Death is a Doorway

[Note: I am including the below full text of a lucid dream experience that Diane Rousseau shared with me. In describing the details of her dream, Diane wrote it within the context of her father's personal spiritual beliefs. As I have emphasized about beliefs throughout this book, these are just his beliefs, in this case bumping up against a more expansive reality. You may not share those beliefs, but I am sharing Diane's experiences with you because of its personal persuasiveness in conveying a father and daughter overcoming the fear of death together.]

"Death is a Doorway"

a true experience
September 23, 1982
by Diane M. Rousseau, PhD
In Loving Memory of John
from a lucid experience, notes taken 09-23-1982

Foreword

This story was written from a diary entry on September 23, 1982; I have kept it in its original format without editing it so as to keep with the feelings that I had when I had this lucid OBE (out of body) experience at age 30. What is important is the material my Dad shared with me out of love to show that there is a continuance of life after bodily death. Though I had past life memories, it is different when one whom you are very close to passes, as it is all the more intense. My Father wanted to show me (and others) that what is life is living Spirit and the body is a temporary form for lessons in physical incarnation. It is written about my father, John, who at age 65 on July 8, 1982 passed away from Cancer. This story describes my dads last days on earth and his transition from this plane of existence through the many dimensional planes that he experienced. It is about a family man, who out of concern and love for his daughter, wife and family is allowed to communicate a message of hope and comfort to his wife as well as help others pass from this world without fear and trust in the Divine. In his own words, my Dad expresses a Spiritual connection with All That Is, and, an Eternal Loving Divine Presence. He learns regardless of faith, we are all the same and to those who have passed from this earth, life "here" becomes the dream.

The purpose of life is to learn the lessons of love, responsibility and to unfold the heart, while understanding the unity behind all life and experience God within. There is a Supreme Being and ones faith is essential to growth and development as one continues to grow, learn and advance. I hope this personal account helps others and provides insight and comfort as well helps to ease the loss and heal any grief or trauma. I was very close to my Dad and not ready, wanting him to see my life, share with him, and see him enjoy life with us all. I worried he had lost somehow, only to find a healing took place which gave me strength and Faith in starting my own Business in 1982.

Respectfully,

Dr. Diane M. Rousseau LHD, PhD

"Death is a Doorway"

By Diane M. Rousseau
September 23, 1982
Around 4:00 AM, Lucid Experience

During the night I had a conscious lucid dream or experience. I was in the living room of our old house where I had grown up in West Seattle, Washington State. I heard a noise in the kitchen and as I walked from the dining room into the kitchen to see who was in the house, I find myself looking at my Dad! He looked at me and smiled and I ran up and hugged him and while he hugged me back with so much happiness, he then asked me; "do you want a toasted cheese sandwich?" I said, "Don't you know what happened to you and where you are?" He answered with a smile, "Yes, do you?" I replied, "You mean that you know you physically died?" Daddy answered, "Yes, but I did not want to shock you, I didn't know how it would be for us," he added, "it took me awhile; dying wasn't anything like I ever thought or heard of, I'm not dead and it's like a dream for me that I was there on earth or even sick. While I was in the Hospital, I kept having this dream of waking up in another place and feeling good, I wanted to get up and get dressed. I would wake up in the apartment (where they lived at the time of his illness) and I would look out the window and see this beautiful park. I knew this was not the view that we had from the apartment window. Also, there were people dressed in white robes that came to the floor and several of them would come in and ask me how I was. I was so tired and was unable to answer and I would then fall asleep and would wake up back in the hospital."

Remembering how those last days were, I asked, "What did it feel like when you would wake up in the hospital?" Dad said, "I didn't think I was in the hospital, I thought I was home and I couldn't understand why I hurt so bad, I felt frustrated because you and Mama (my Mother) wouldn't let me up; I wanted you to see I was fine, but I was unable to talk." I said, "That must have been confusing, did you feel any pain; they were giving you morphine?" Daddy said, "Yes, I did, but it was more like I was fighting to stay awake and I did not notice the pain so much and then I would fall asleep and wake up at the other beautiful place again.

There would be a beautiful person in white sitting on the edge of the bed who would ask me if I was ready to get up yet. I felt torn and this went on for 3 days, back and forth to both places and I could feel the pain of not wanting to leave you and Mama." (My Dad died of Cancer, which was in several areas on his body; he had just retired and a month later while seeing the Doctor, they noticed a lump on the left side of his neck. The lump was biopsied and was diagnosed as Cancer, which had metastasized into the lymph nodes. My Dad passed 5 months later at age 65.)

I asked him what dying felt like and if he felt scared. "No", daddy answered, "it's like falling asleep and dreaming. In the last two days, I started to feel like the hospital was the dream and that I was really fine. I felt so good and happy in the other place and I didn't want to have that "dream" anymore; of being in that hospital and feeling so sick. On the last day while I was half asleep at the hospital, I heard Mama tell me that is was "ok to let go." So I just let go and then woke up immediately at the other place. It looked like the bedroom of our apartment, except that a park was right out the window and BeBe (their tortoiseshell cat that has passed some years earlier) was on the bed and I felt so good so I got up and got dressed." I said, "You mean Missy don't you?" (Their present cat was also a Tortoiseshell Persian) And Daddy answered, "No, our first Persian cat. Then the people in white came in the room and asked me how I felt, and I said fine!" I asked daddy how many of the people came into his room at that time, what they looked like and did he know or recognize any of them. He answered, "three, and they were all dressed in white robes with long sleeves and their robe came to the floor, they were beautiful, light haired and were of light and had light around them, they were young and did not look either male or female; he said, "I did not recognize them and that they were very happy when they saw I that was awake and dressed!"

Daddy then described to me how he had changed out of the hospital gown and had put on his favorite blue Pendleton plaid shirt, his tan pants, and favorite slippers that were by the bed. I looked at him and noticed that he looked younger and his eyes were soft and the look on his face was more peaceful then I had ever seen, then, I glanced down and saw he had his wedding ring on and I asked him about it. He answered, "of course I do, it's my wedding ring, it's because of the way I feel about it and Mama that it is on me." Then he told me that after a short while he started to feel tired and asked them about it. The Beings or Angels told him that this was normal and due to his illness and passing and that later on he would be fine; they then said they would come back later after he had rested. So Dad recounted that then he went back down the hall into the bedroom and described how he felt when he laid back down and how good it felt and how good he felt inside; very peaceful with no sadness or fear. He then told me he heard them in his mind and felt them. He realized that they had not ever verbally spoken to him, that it was inside his mind that he heard and felt them; they were individual and distinct. His cat BeBe was still lying on the bed, and he told me he called her saying, "come here cat," she then came over to him and curled up next to him purring, they both fell asleep.

Dad then said he "dreamed" his life; the *dream* began from the moment he died in the hospital and went all the way back to his first memory as a baby. He told me he re-lived every moment. He said that he felt all his thoughts and feelings acutely as well as those of the people around him, he was witnessing all the experiences; he said it was like being in a movie while watching it at the same time. He told me from his experiences that each person is responsible for their thoughts, speech and actions, but most importantly, their intentions. He said, "You know Diane, what you "think" is more important than what you do; for it is in the mind where it all begins." He then pointed to his head and said with a smile, "but this keeps you from doing too much about what you think." He said he feels us when we think of him and that he can also hear us talking about or to him. He said to tell Mama that she should read the "*dream*" book that I had given him to read before he became very ill and though it left out a lot, it was the only thing he had ever read that came close to describing what he was experiencing.

I had given him the Book: "What Dreams May

Come" By Richard Matheson, because I wanted to give him something that he might find helpful and interesting that was also similar to my own experiences; I had also given my parents other Spiritual books. Daddy wanted me to tell Mama that she could see him too, that for a time, people who have recently passed to the other side can communicate with us and see us. Then, he said, they have to get on with their personal growth and gain understanding of their life, relationships and with more knowledge they are able to make better decisions for the future. He said that learning never stops and that there are Temples and Universities for those who want to learn and for when they feel they are ready to more deeply understand their previous life to make better decisions. Each life is very important and has great meaning, even if one does not see it for them selves in that life or understands this about others.

He now looked at me with soft eyes and seemed to notice something and stated, "You have been unhappy haven't you?" I answered that I had and that I had not really been ready for him to leave, although I was being strong for my Mom, I missed him very much. It is hard to watch your parent or a loved one who is suffering with a severe illness; it especially bothered me because my dad had worked hard all his life with very few vacations. He had just retired 6 months earlier before he passed only to find out that he had Cancer. It was all over his body and had been there for a while and when he was diagnosed, the Doctors at that time said there was not much that could be done. I had wanted to see him have some time for enjoying life and also for all of us to have more free time together. I was 30 years old and was going to miss him as he was the closest to me, he had believed in me as did my Mentor Charlie and the loss in my life was for many reasons and I was also very worried about my mom, and for others who I knew were close to him. Living in the present is so important; one never knows when the chance to come together will end.

I asked Daddy if he felt lonely or missed my Mother and I or any of his relative or friends on earth. I wanted to know if he had seen any of his friends or family members or others he had known that had passed earlier. With that he told me that he "never felt lonely because he always feels us and those he loves", that he felt at peace because we are always connected in the heart, the soul, and that this is true for everyone with deep relationships. He said that he "would not see any of the people in his life who did not love him, only those with whom he had good relationships and friendships; where there was mutual love and caring and only good memories and experiences are remembered." He told me that he "did not really remember or feel the bad memories from his past life anymore after he had awakened from his dream-life review experience." He felt that "life on earth was a dream and it was only a small part of who and what one is." He told me "I could talk to him anytime and that when I did, he will feel and hear me and to tell this to Mama; for it would help her as well as others whom I shared this experience with." He added that "Prayers are very important for those who pass, especially in the first 3 - 4 days, because they do feel our sorrow, it is best not to pull on them as they feel our pain. Being with them and giving love is critical while they are passing as well as the room being quiet; being silent, praying and meditating helps the atmosphere and their feelings to be at peace."

Daddy told me for now he "would not see anyone that had passed that he knew; that this was his time for healing, happiness and for his reflections on the good of his life and what he had learned as well as what he felt that he still needed to learn." He said "the Beings advised him on the importance of these reflections, so one is never alone during this time and that they are there and that his cat BeBe was still with him and all the other pets that my parents had owned and loved who had passed to this side; all were there and very happy being together again."

I asked him at this point "what happened to him after he had re-lived his life in the Life Review experience?" He said, "That when it was over, he got up and felt better, he was happier than he ever was in life on earth. That where he was now living, time did not exist for him, but in our time it took about 5 or 6 weeks before he could advance to this next point. He said he "rested a lot in the "apartment" and that the Beings in white watched over him all the time and kept him company. Though he experienced no suffering or pain, the resting he required had to do with being so sick before he died and that this was true for others who had long illnesses." I asked him "what happened when he got up?" He told me that he walked out of the bedroom and down the hall and was greeted by several Beings in white; they smiled at him and said in his mind, "How are you John!?" He said they felt like love, and though they did not give him their names, he would recognize them by sight and feelings. He said, "they were very happy to see him up and around and one asked him if he realized what had happened to him and if he fully understood where he was. He thought to himself that he was not sure, but before he could answer, another one of the Being's told him that he was in what we would call "Heaven" and that Heaven had many levels to it. These "Heavens" were particular to ones understandings and beliefs." He said right then, "he thought of the book I had given him again, and as he later walked around the beautiful park and grounds, he remembered it was similar to what was described in the book and that it really helped him in the beginning." Daddy said where he was (implying that some places have different environments) that there was no "night", no shadows or darkness where he was now and that it was always light there; and though he did not see the sun like we do, everything was lit up by itself." He told me he, "was very happy and that this was only the beginning of his experiences and learning." He added that the reason he now stayed in our old house was because he had been happier there than any other places that he had remembered in his earthly life. As I looked around, I noticed how perfect and beautiful everything was; it was as he had always talked about, expansions and colors and thought of how he had said he wanted it to be even though he was unable to have it look that way when he lived in it on earth.

Daddy said "they" give you what you are used for awhile and things change around you the more you realize that you do not really need anything in the way people do when they are on earth. Sleep, food and habits as well as all human functions fall away when one is ready for it. He said, "it is different for each person and ones Faith did not seem to matter in the same way, it was a guide to life. He said he felt love everywhere and that he could learn anything he wanted to and was able to go anywhere he wanted; it was up to what he "thought and felt the most strongly about." He also knew he would reincarnate again eventually, but that was a long time away for him and that for now he would "wait" for Mama.

I felt very happy inside for him; I was relieved and felt tears on my face. I was grateful to have this experience and to be able to see how happy he was and to know he was alright and where he wanted to be;

even waiting for my Mother did not bother him at all, for he felt her all the time even if she did not realize it. He said he knew I was ok, as we had shared the spiritual part of life; this was my relationship to him. Though in my heart he would always be "daddy" to me, I knew we in other times had been many things; ours was an entirely spiritual soul connection. He was selfless and cared very much for others during his life, which I had always admired and I knew this was our real connection and how as a child I was inspired by him. He had been a Designer of Freeways, started several Business, ran for City Council, was a policeman and then went into the Fire Department, became a Journeyman Electrician, and the last part of his life he was a Crane Operator at a Shipyard and really enjoyed being by the water in Puget Sound; he especially liked working with others.

I started to feel a tugging sensation and knew I was going to have to return to my sleeping body. I did not "take off at random" as my spiritual mentor Charlie Lutes had advised me not to do in 1974; instead, I waited for learning experiences as Charlie suggested when they needed to come and so knew this was an experience given though Grace for a purpose. Daddy held me again and said, "Now don't forget to tell Mama about what we talked about!" I looked at him with happiness and said, "I won't daddy!" The bliss between us stayed and a mist came over me as he faded away and I softly returned to my sleeping body.

I immediately got up and wrote down my experience. Later that morning, I phoned my Mother and shared with her the experience I had. She was quiet and I realized that though I was sharing with her and was so happy, that I was not sure if she believed me or not (she would not say), I *do* know the experience gave her great comfort and much to think about.

Addendum

It was not much time later that she too read the "dream" book about the afterlife that I had given them; she also began to read other books and one time she told me she thought she had seen daddy too. One of the last books that I shared with her before she passed in 1998 was "The Inner Life" by C. W. Leadbeater. I wrote this Story and titled it as daddy asked, as he wanted me to share his experience to help others. I hope it has brought some insight for those who are suffering, lost or alone. We really are never alone; the Almighty sends Messengers and Guides to always be with us even if we do not always see them. It is about love and the growth of the soul and what we learn here and from each other. What might seem lost or incomplete is recognized and another chance is given to be together again and either heal or enjoy what could not happen due to an illness or early passing. Being of service to others is most important and is essential to growth. Later in my life I was overjoyed that my Dad saw my work, as we often wonder if they know. When I last saw him he looked about 23 years of age, red hair, tall and was present when I had spoke earlier at a Conference. This is heartening as I have had other experiences with people who have passed and it is those we have the strongest Soul connection with that keeps us together as we go forth on the journey; there really is life Eternal.

NOTE:

This was a lucid experience; my father wanted people to know by his letting go, that he did experience a peaceful passing; he experienced no pain at all and had no fear. He also wanted me to put this experience down on paper so it would be shared with others.

Copyright © 1982, 2006, 2016 Diane M. Rousseau LHD, PhD

About the Foundation

The Overcoming the Fear of Death Foundation is a nonprofit 501(c)(3) organization located in Austin, Texas, and is qualified under U.S. federal law by the IRS. Its mission is to help people, regardless of their belief system, overcome their fear of death and related fears, so they can free up that energy to live more productive, enjoyable lives.

Donations to support the Foundation's work around the world can be made via the website at:

www.OvercomingTheFearOfDeath.org

Donations are tax deductible to the extent allowed by the IRS.

The Foundation also has a FaceBook page at:

www.facebook.com/OvercomingTheFearOfDeath

About the Author

Kelvin H. Chin is the Executive Director and Founder of both the Overcoming the Fear of Death Foundation and the nonprofit TurningWithin.org. Working with audiences on death and dying issues since the 1980's, Kelvin has taught numerous seminars for the healthcare industry, was a state-certified Long Term Care Ombudsman for the California Department of Aging, and a co-founder of the Center For Medical Ethics and Mediation.

Bringing greater clarity to his client's thinking in their personal and business life is something Kelvin has applied throughout his 40-year career, including teaching meditation worldwide to more than 1,000 people since the 1970's in schools, businesses, the U.S. Army and at West Point. Kelvin also formerly held CMO roles at AmLaw100 law firms, and was a VP for the American Arbitration Association.

Kelvin was born in Boston, raised in Norwood, Massachusetts, and has since lived and worked in 6 countries. He has delivered more than 2,000 presentations worldwide.

While at Dartmouth College, he studied at the Université de Strasbourg, France. He is a graduate of Dartmouth, Yale Graduate School and Boston College Law School, and is the father of two artistically talented children.

Kelvin can be contacted at
www.OvercomingTheFearOfDeath.org
and followed on Twitter at
@KelvinHChin

HOW TO GIFT THIS BOOK
To a Friend or a Loved One…

To get a copy of this book mailed to your home,
or to get an e-book or audiobook downloaded now…
(Kelvin does the audiobook voice reading)

HERE'S HOW...
Simply SCAN this QR Code:

OR

Go to this Link:

http://www.OvercomingTheFearOfDeath.org/books

To download the QR code app for your mobile phone, simply follow these steps:

1. Open your mobile app store (App Store, Google Play, Windows Marketplace, etc.)

2. Search for "QR Code Readers"

3. Download the free QR Reader to your phone, and Open it

4. Hold your camera over the above QR Code in this book, and Scan it

5. Enter your information to order your book!